Growing to Eat Italian Style

From Seed to Plate

PAOLO ARRIGO

Photography by Steve Lee

SIMON & SCHUSTER
A CBS COMPANY

A cookbook from **Seeds of Italy**

First published in Great Britain by Simon & Schuster UK Ltd. 2009. A CBS Company

Text copyright © Paolo Arrigo 2009
Simon & Schuster UK Ltd, 1st Floor, 222 Gray's Inn Road, London WC1X 8HB

1 3 5 7 9 10 8 6 4 2

Text Design: Jane Humphrey *Photography:* Steve Lee *Styling:* Jo Harris *Home economy:* Sue Ashworth
Printed and bound in China ISBN 978 1 84737 307 6

Recipe credits: Jean-Christophe Novelli, *Everyday Novelli* (Headline Book Publishing 2008): © p 15 Childhood Baked Stuffed Tomatoes. Mary Contini, Valvona & Crolla Italian Delicatessen, Edinburgh, *Dear Francesca: An Italian Journey of Recipes Recounted with Love* (Ebury Press 2003): © p 18 Fresh Tomato Sauce. Chef Maurizio Morelli, Latium, London: © p 24 Salad of Prawns with 'Lattuga' Sauce, Basil and Orange Segments. Gennaro Contaldo, *Gennaro's Italian Year* (Headline Book Publishing 2006): © p 35 Salad of Radicchio, Pear, Chestnuts and Gorgonzola. Hugh Fearnley-Whittingstall, *The River Cottage Year* (Hodder & Stoughton Ltd 2005): © p 36 Grilled Radicchio with Melted Cheese. Jimmy Doherty ('Jimmy's Farm'), *A Taste of the Country by Jimmy Doherty* (Michael Joseph, 2007). Recipes and text copyright © Jimmy Doherty, 2007. Reproduced by permission of Penguin Books Ltd: © p 38 Dandelion and Bacon Salad. Let's Go Italian (www.letsgoitalian.com): © p 53 Cirillini Pasta with Tomato and Courgette. Giuseppe Silvestri, Head Chef, Harrods: © p 53 Stuffed Courgette Flowers. Ursula Ferrigno, *Truly Italian* (Mitchell Beazley 2003): © p 54 Sun-dried Courgettes with Mint and Garlic. Rose Gray, The River Cafe, London: © p 54 Zucchini Trifolati. Neil Haydock, Executive Chef, Fifteen, Cornwall: © p 58 Marina di Chioggia Caponata. Lina Stores, 18 Brewer Street, Soho: © p 61 Pumpkin Rice; © p 221 Bread Cake. Antony Worrall Thompson: © p 66 Roasted Peperonata. Marco Centonze, MD Peperoncino Ltd: © p 70 Stuffed Chilli Peppers. Aldo Zilli: © p 78 Plaice Fillets Rolled in Cabbage with Prosecco Sauce. Cyrus Rustom Todiwala, Executive Chef / Patron, Café Spice Namasté, London: © p 80 Thimi Tarkari Masala. Giancarlo and Katie Caldesi, *Return to Tuscany – Recipes from a Tuscan Cookery School* (BBC Books 2006): © p 83 Ribollita. By courtesy of Franchi Sementi spa, Bergamo: © p 84 Orecchiette e Cima di Rape; © p 167 Sarajevo soup; © p 173 Tortelli with Ricotta and Greens. Country House Montali, *The Vegeterranean* (Simon & Schuster UK Ltd): © p 98 Porri al Montasio; © p 105 Broad Bean Purée; © p 128 Gnocchi di Patate; © p 130 Gateau di Patate. Andy Needham, Zafferano, London: © p 118 Risi Bisi; © p 120 Marinated Artichokes with Burrata and Peas. Franco Taruschio, *100 Great Pasta Dishes* (Kyle Cathie 2005); © p 137 Tagliolini with Artichokes and Parma Ham. Andrea Falter, from her recipe collection Traditional German Cooking © p 146 Asparagus with Bolzano Sauce. Giorgio Locatelli, *Made in Italy* (Fourth Estate 2008): © p 150 Caponata. Jim, Head Chef, The Granville, Lower Hardres, Kent: © p 152 Beetroot Carpaccio. Dan De Gustibus, De Gustibus (award-winning artisan bread makers), Borough Market, London: © p 154 Crunchy Carrot Loaf with Mustard and Thyme. Rose Prince, *The New English Table: Good Cooking That will Not Cost the Earth* (Fourth Estate 2008): © p 160 Well-dressed Raw Roots. Chef Amy Hunt, Oak and Glass, Weston-super-Mare: © p 194 Roasted Tomato and Fennel Soup. Alex Beard, Personal Chef, based in Cardiff but will travel anywhere with you! www.yourchefis.com: © p 164 Sea Bass and Roasted Fennel with Coriander, Tomato and Wild Rocket Dressing. Elisabeth Luard, *Truffles* (Frances Lincoln 2006): © p 197 Cheese Fondue with Truffles. Camisa Delicatessen, Old Compton St, Soho: © p 202 Mushroom and Fontina Salad; © p 202 Mushroom Risotto.
Photo Credits: p 4 courtesy of Eugene Cook; p 144 © Verusca Calabria; all other family photographs courtesy of Paolo Arrigo. Every effort has been made to obtain permissions and assign the correct copyright to all contributers and apologies are made for any unintentional omissions or errors.

Acknowledgements: I would like to thank in particular mu   es; my wife Alex, who I love with all my heart and who supports me t   ister-in-law Marisa, who can never do enough for us; my grandparent   I am like a son; my aunties Angelina, Annamari', Fiorina, Maria, Angela a   aetano and Lorenzo, who all watched me grow up; Lina Castagna in c   reserving; the many chefs and restaurateurs who have supported me w   community, where everyone looks out for each other; Mr Franchi, wh   lshake, trust and respect; the garden centres and delis that had the vis   s; and you, the reader, who buys Franchi seeds, grows your own veg, wa   noney too. Life is about relationships and my relationships with all of you (y

contents

This photo shows the 'Sagra', held on the first Sunday after July 16th
and the oldest continuing running festival in London. A Catholic procession dedicated to Our Lady of Mount Carmel,
it always attracts thousands, who come to see the floats and enjoy the Italian food and atmosphere.

introduzione

INTRODUCTION

When I was thirteen I played truant from school with a classmate. We hid out in Chorley Woods, and during that day I found two beautiful porcini mushrooms. I couldn't just leave them so I took them home. Every bit of me knew that if I did this I would get found out, yet a mysterious passion within convinced me it was still the right thing to do.

Well, it wasn't every day that I went to school and came home with porcini mushrooms, so I was rumbled. This story really highlights Italian life, even in Britain, because on the one hand I got a hiding I will always remember, but on the other hand we had porcini risotto for dinner, which I ate with pleasure while twitching around on my sore bum on the chair and with great satisfaction, because I had found the porcini! I knew my dad was secretly proud of me, certainly not for playing truant but because I had done a very 'Italian' thing.

Someone once said that Italy is not a country, it is a way of life. A large part of this way of life is food and all things related. Shops and offices close for lunch between one and four, bars sell more espressos than beer, and a good night out is judged by what and how much you ate, rather than drank – although we drink well too. The last two weddings I've attended in Italy each consisted of twenty-six courses. Every course is greeted with a cheer from the diners, full of as much excitement as six-year-olds when the birthday cake is brought out.

Italians have had great influence all over the world on what and how we eat. It started with the Romans, masters of trade, who distributed produce from one part of their empire to another. They introduced to the British Isles, amongst other things, onions, basil, figs, cardoons, rocket, chervil, leeks, carrots, asparagus, endives, chicory, melons, walnuts, bay, garlic, lavender, parsley, apricots, pears, rosemary, sage, thyme, borage, cucumbers and vines. And now, Italian emigration has been such over the years that the number of Italians living outside Italy equals the population within the country.

In present-day Italy, many people still grow their own and practically everyone who cooks, grows, and vice versa. If you buy a flat in Milan, it will come with two things – a garage, because you drive, and an allotment, because you grow. That's that – punto e basta! Italian dishes tend to be uncomplicated, often of peasant origin, but using the freshest and most genuine ingredients. These ingredients are so important that most Italians will still shop daily for their produce in bustling markets brimming with unshelled borlotti beans, tomatoes of every shape and size and meaty peppers almost as big as rugby balls, and in shops that offer salami and regional meats of every description, cheese counters that fill an entire fridge, olives, dried pulses and wonderful breads. But priority is always given to whichever vegetable is in season in the orto, or veg patch.

Recently we exhibited our seeds at the Dolce Vita show at Olympia, a show for Italian companies only. What really impressed me was the pride the producers conveyed to their customers. The mozzarella-maker will tell you everything about that humble mozzarella, how it was made, the ingredients, the process, how best to conserve it, how to enjoy it. The show was full of artisans like this – every product known in minute detail from the seed to the plate, and this is typical of an Italian high street. In my wife's town near Venice, for example, the local cheese is called Asiago, and there is an Asiago shop. It sells nothing else – no Gorgonzola, no Toma, no mozzarella... just Asiago, smoked, fresh, aged, flavoured with herbs.

And this is the premise behind the book: it's all about hand-me-downs, tradition, a word I love with extra amore. Why do I go mushroom-picking? Because my dad took me, his dad took him and so on. And now I take my son, who is three and already knows some of the varieties he shouldn't be picking – a start at least.

Tradition holds true for the way you grow the veg, cook the recipes and eat the dishes. Many of the basic dishes I cook now I cooked with my parents, my cousins, aunts and uncles, or at small village 'festas', where other people taught me their techniques and recipes. I may have had to look up the specifics the first few times, but I had done them before indirectly, so knew what to expect, how it should taste, look and feel. And I was accustomed to a culture where food is celebrated and enjoyed. So much pride and effort went into a dish that it always tasted better. Eating was a celebration every time.

This book has been written from an Anglo-Italian point of view, as one of many people born here of Italian parentage. I am not a chef, but both my brother Marco and I have been raised in the Italian way – in the kitchen, at the table, in the garden and in my father's deli. Our family always had proper food and always ate together. By proper food, I mean food that has been cooked from scratch. When Mum and Dad were skint, they bought what they could afford, but a good cook in my opinion isn't someone who can make a meal with a fridge full of great produce, but someone who can make something out of nothing, using ingredients they have to hand.

Tradition and family life have shaped my brother and me into who we are today, and many of our best memories involve food in one way or another: scraping the cake batter from the inside of a bowl with Mum, mushroom-picking and helping in the deli with Dad, cooking a whole pig with my zia Fiorina, picnics with my parents when they were young and had no money and countless special and nostalgic meals and gatherings. Probably no coincidence then that I sell vegetable seeds and Marco sells illy coffee!

I know my onions, so to speak, on Italian vegetables because of my company and because it's also my passion. My brother is a company director for illy coffee – the best coffee in the world, in my opinion. Illy coffee is his passion and if the competition offered him a million quid, he couldn't sell their stuff. You're either passionate about what you do or you shouldn't do it. I started Seeds of Italy by accident. I wanted some Italian seed packets to sell in our family deli in West Hendon. So I went through my seed box in the shed and I had twelve different Italian seed brands, but only one had both some English and a picture on the packet. Fate had fortuitously guided me to the Franchi seed brand, which is the oldest family-run seed company in the world and one of the most respected. They still commission the vast majority (over 90 per cent) of their own vegetable seed locally in Italy rather than buying it from the lowest bidder.

Anyway, I had no intention of distributing these at the time and was happy to be the only deli in the UK with a range of Italian vegetable seeds! Then a friend, who also owns a deli, asked where I got the stand and whether he could have one. Only then did a lightbulb switch on. I originally intended offering the seeds only to Italian delis – it didn't even occur to me at that point that garden centres sold seeds. The seeds were stored in my garage, where I had installed a portable aircon unit to keep the temperature down in summer; a far cry from our warehouse unit now. My first seed order came to £250, which I borrowed from my dad, who thought I was mad. With the Franchi seed brand now growing (no pun intended) rapidly, my passion has grown at the same rate, and I hope this comes across in this book. I have never worked so hard in my life, but there is satisfaction in sharing something you love and practising what you preach.

Cookery books are just people handing down their knowledge to others, and this is all I wish to do. I've tried to explain how to prepare and use the ingredients and to give advice on growing different varieties, but in the same way that recipes differ from person to person, so can the tips given. Italian cookbooks work on the premise that you can cook already and that they are merely giving you inspiration or ideas on what to cook. Often they don't give quantities, because, of course, you will know how many tomatoes to use for two, four or six people! I've tried to be a little more helpful. I've also included some sayings and proverbs. Some of them are just for fun, but I feel that they reflect Italian life, referring to food, religion, family or farming. Some I've heard in Piedmont, others are from a superb book by Tino Richelmy called *Proverbi Piemontese*.

I want to end this introduction back with my family: my two grandmothers, Nonna Emilia in Italy and Nonna Angela in London. Nonna Angela lived in Britain most of her life – they had a fish and chip shop in south London and then she worked in the Hyde Park Hotel kitchens along with many other Piedmontese and Italians. She made the best stuffed onions and ravioli in little stampe or moulds, all by hand, one by one. Nonna Emilia lived through the tough war years in Italy and could make a meal out of nothing – polenta with milk, peaches stuffed with

amaretti biscuits, dandelion salad. She would get up at 7 a.m., have breakfast then start preparing and cooking lunch. Lunch finished, she would clear up, and after a rest would start on dinner.

Nonna Emilia always finished every meal by saying, 'E anche oggi abbiamo mangiato' (even today we've managed to eat). Whatever she made, however simple, it was outstanding and it tasted great because she always used great ingredients. I carry this passion for genuine ingredients, and it's the reason for 'From Seed to Plate'. The name says it all. I hope I can get across my passion to you in such a way that you can experience and enjoy it as much as me. P.A.

In memoria di mio padre,
Cavaliere Vincenzo Arrigo

Regionality

Italy is a country of regions and every region could well be a different country. Even the dialects change from town to town, and sometimes even from village to village. My mother says that my father's family used to call her 'the foreigner' because her family came from Ivrea, a town only twenty miles away from his village. Like these dialects, there are often subtle changes in the regional dishes. I've heard heated discussions on what ingredients should go into a particular dish, when they should be added, what varieties to use and how long to cook the dish.

Recently, I went to a transport café when driving through Biella, and I was served a fixed-price meal of fresh local salami with homemade bread, pasta with a roasted tomato and courgette sauce to die for, veal escalopes with a good quality side of local seasonal veg, chips, a glass of wine and a coffee – all for ten euros. On the motorway the day before I had stopped for a meal fearing the worst. In the motorway restaurant they were serving only regional dishes made with ingredients sourced from Aosta, Piedmont and Lombardy. It was restaurant-quality food and this is the norm, not the exception.

Italian food is regional because the varieties are regional. Italy is almost unique in that it has managed to preserve most of its regional varieties. Thus there are different varieties of courgette from Bologna, Genoa, Florence, Rome, Milan, Naples, Sarzana, Piacenza, Nizza, Albenga, Friuli and Sicily, and these are just the ones I know of! Every region will then have its own recipe for cooking its particular variety. There are many vegetarian recipes in Italy, but not because Italians don't like meat, but because of the exceptional quality of the regional varieties. This is really why Italian food is so interesting and diverse; using the right variety is a key to replicating the dish perfectly. For example, you could use any borlotti bean to make the famous Venetian dish of Pasta e Fagioli but, to re-create it faithfully, use the Lamon borlotti variety. This particular variety hails from Venice and is little known outside the Veneto region. Make this dish with the right variety and you will be transported to that trip to Italy when you first tasted it.

I remember once asking my aunt in Venice why she always grew the yellow, knobbly, ugly Venetian courgette instead of (normal) green ones. She said that she had seen green courgettes but didn't use them because they look funny! Zia Maria also practises a lot of old gardening techniques – 'we've always done it this way' she said to me once when sowing her potatoes on a certain saint's day. But many of these 'old wives' tales' do have elements of truth in them and do work, although it's not always understood why. Take the practice of sowing by the moons. The general rule is that things you grow above ground you should sow with a growing (waxing) moon, and things that grow below ground, with a shrinking (waning) moon. Some people may scoff, but who are we to do so when people have been doing this for thousands of years?

The inhabitants of each region are fiercely proud of their roots. Part of that pride includes preserving the seed of their beloved regional varieties and passing them down from father to son. The following cities or regions have their own regional vegetable varieties. It will never be exact – sometimes a region's claim to a variety is disputed – but it is a pretty impressive list.

Abruzzo: cucumber, garlic

Adorno: chilli

Alba: white pregiato truffle, strawberry

Albenga: squash, asparagus, bean

Alto Adige: cauliflower

Asti: pepper (2), celery, Savoy cabbage

Aqualagna: white pregiato truffle

Bari: cucumber, Swiss chard

Bergamo: onion, escarole, endive, pepper

Bologna: courgette

Brindisi: Catalogna chicory

Calabria: broccoli, chilli, pepper

Cantalupo: melon

Castelfranco: chicory

Chiavari: chicory

Chioggia: chicory (2), beetroot, carrot, pumpkin

Cosenza: melon

Cuneo: pepper

Faenza: courgette

Florence: tomato, onion (2), courgette, aubergine, escarole

Friuli: courgette

Genova: onion, courgette, basil, tomato

Jesi: cauliflower

Lecce: cucumber

Liguria: tomato, purple asparagus, courgette

Lodi: turnip

Lombardia: pepper

Lusia: chicory (2)

Macerata: cima di rapa, cauliflower

Manduria: cucumber, tomato

Mantova: chicory, Savoy cabbage, fennel

Milan: onion, courgette, turnip, chicory

Montebianco: fennel

Naples: parsley, pumpkin (2), courgette, basil, pepper, chilli, aubergine, cabbage (2), Savoy cabbage (3), cauliflower (4), endive, fennel, turnip (2), tomato (5+), escarole, lettuce, radish (2), celery, melon

Nizza Monferato: endive

Padana: pumpkin

Pancalieri: endive (2), mint

Parma: fennel, onion

Piacenza: courgette, pumpkin, garlic

Piemonte: hazelnut, blueberry, bean, mint, endive

Puglia: cucumber, chicory, Catalogna chicory, escarole

Romagna: artichoke, aubergine, cardoon, celery

Rome: tomato (2), lettuce (6+), courgette, cauliflower, endive, fennel, aubergine, artichoke, aubergine

Saluggia: borlotti bean

Sardegna: radish, chilli

Sarno: fennel, Swiss chard, broccoli, cima di rapa (3), lettuce

Sarzana: courgette

Savona: onion

Sicily: tomato, squash, cauliflower, courgette, basil

Soncino: chicory

Sulmona: garlic

Trento: lettuce, apple

Treviso: radicchio (3)

Trieste: chicory, courgette

Tropea: onion (2)

Turin: celery

Tuscany: kale, onion (2), courgette

Venice: celeriac, borlotti bean, French bean (4), chicory, garlic

Verona: radicchio (3), Savoy cabbage

Vigevano: borlotti bean (2)

coltivando verdure e le erbe aromatiche

GROWING VEGETABLES AND HERBS

If there is a vegetable-growing and a food-loving gene, we Italians have it! The culture is ingrained in us from birth and throughout life.

It's not uncommon in Italy for schools, offices, factories, even police stations and hospitals to have an orto. An apartment will have tomatoes and basil growing on the balcony alongside the ivy geraniums. This came home to me recently when I was travelling by train from Biella to Portogruaro. At almost every station we pulled into, I noticed an immaculately tended trackside orto, brimming with deep red, misshapen beef tomatoes, courgettes, radicchio and other leaves. Even at Milan central station, in August, you'll see amazing tomato orto in between the tracks as the train pulls out, the drivers picking tomatoes to eat with bread or cheese.

In the UK there has been a resurgence of vegetable-growing in recent years, partly due to TV chefs using the freshest and best ingredients, partly due to gardening programmes and to agricultural issues, GM and the organic movement. Magazines have played a part too, with the result that allotments, which were overgrown ten years ago, now have four-year waiting lists.

There is also an increased interest in different seed varieties, especially from Italy. But don't be misled. Some of the cheap 'Italian'-style seed packets contain nothing of the sort. My mother howled with laughter at the description on the back of one packet, which described the most famous Neapolitan pepper, the Frigitello, as being used to make Peperonata. In fact, the pepper is the size of a chilli pepper – you'd need about 200 to make just one dish of Peperonata; in Italy, Frigitello peppers are simply pan-fried in olive oil, seasoned with salt and eaten with a beer. We started Seeds of Italy through frustration at not being able to find Neapolitan Bolloso basil, courgettes from Milan or beans from Venice, and seeing San Marzano tomatoes only in tins. Even when you found them, you had to pay through the nose for a radicchio from Verona.

Will these varieties grow in the UK? A tomato seed will germinate at the same temperature in Siberia or Saint Lucia. It's just the growing on that differs, so treat the seed as you would a similar domestic variety and the plant will prosper. Don't forget that two-thirds of Italy is alpine, with the Alps and Dolomite mountains in the north and the Apennines running down the middle, with winter temperatures as low as -20°C. Some lettuce and radicchio varieties, for example, can withstand temperatures of -15°C, so with Italian seed you can grow more, not less.

People ask: 'Will it taste the same as if it was grown in Italy?' This assumes that the soil in Italy is the same from Sicily to Aosta. My soil and conditions in Harrow are different from my mum's in North Harrow! In many ways Italy is a difficult place to grow veg, as it can get to -30°C in the north and +50°C in the south. Britain is far more temperate and reliable. If we have a better summer in London than in Turin, which is quite often the case, then our Cuor di Bue tomatoes from Liguria will do better than the same tomatoes in Turin. It is impossible to generalize. What is important is the variety. A cauliflower di Sicilia is harvested until the end of November, a cauliflower Romanesco is harvested until the end of January, and a cauliflower of Verona until the end of March – a difference of five months.

A seed wants to grow – its whole purpose is reproduction and it will usually succeed despite your efforts. If you chuck a handful of seeds over your shoulder into the earth, most won't make it, but something will probably come up. Once when I was stuck in traffic, I put my hand in my pocket to get a sweet and came across a damaged pack of radicchio Rossa di Treviso. As my car inched up the road , I chucked the seed on to the grass verge. Some weeks later I went the same way, and amidst the rubbish there stood a solitary radicchio plant. Of course, there's more to it than that, in cultivating and producing a top-quality vegetable to eat.

If you are new to growing veggies, start with a pot of herbs or rocket. What could be better than picking fresh basil from the windowsill to tear on to a tomato, or Neapolitan parsley leaves chopped and added to chopped eggs and mayo for a sandwich? Then graduate to a cutting lettuce in a tub – very easy, tasty and a lot cheaper than buying a bag of 'ready washed'. Some things are easier to grow than others. Cutting lettuce, rocket, Swiss chard, parsley, bush tomatoes, lamb's lettuce, spinach and beans are very easy. These are the ones you sow directly into the ground. As long as you keep them watered (but not wet), nature will do the rest. All you have to do is harvest them and enjoy. Other species are intermediate level: courgettes, pumpkins, squashes, peas, cordon tomatoes, aubergines and peppers (which will need a greenhouse in the UK), onions, lettuce heads, kale... Sow these in trays first and then transplant when there is no further risk of frost. The trickier ones to grow from seed are carrots, brassicas like cabbages and cauliflowers, okra, fennel, asparagus, rhubarb, some cucumbers and radishes. With some, pests are a particular problem, others need particular conditions or are quirky.

Don't be too rigid with gardening. If it says on the packet to sow until the end of June and it's the 5th of July, it'll probably still grow successfully. And it's a mistake to think that once Easter is over it's too late to sow anything. There are more herbs and veggies you can grow after May than before. The British are the best in the world at sowing vegetables in spring, and the worst at sowing throughout the year (with the exception of sowing broad beans and planting garlic in the autumn). We even cover our allotments in the winter instead of sowing or harvesting from them. In Italy, because there are hardy varieties (as well as Mediterranean ones), there is always something to be sown or harvested, not just in spring and summer. One example is lettuce – a neighbour used to sow lettuces once or twice and by July had eaten them all. I was still sowing in October while he was preparing to cover his allotment with plastic.

Every year is different: 2002 was the wettest on record and was not good for tomatoes; 2003 was the hottest on record and tomatoes were fantastic; 2004 was very mixed and was just all right for tomatoes, although they were late in the season. Similarly no two gardens are the same. If your neighbour grows great carrots, it doesn't follow that you will too. He/she may have been adding compost for thirty years, and your soil might be full of building rubble! So use the information in this book as a guide to discover, by trial and error, what you're good at.

pomodori

TOMATOES

The Italian for tomatoes is 'pomodori', literally translated as 'golden apples'. Italian tomatoes are considered to be some of the best in the world, especially plum varieties for cooking, and the Italians really have a love affair with the golden apple.

Although tomatoes originated in Mexico and Peru and weren't imported to Europe until after the Americas were discovered, the Italians, and to a lesser degree the Spanish, really do the tomato well. In the sixteenth century the tomato was a small, bitter, yellow thing (hence the 'golden' in its name), worlds apart from the juicy sweet red globe we now know – depending on where you buy your tomatoes that is! It is through breeding over the centuries that the tomato has changed so much.

They are so versatile: they can become the base for rich sauces, they can be made into 'passata' or just eaten raw in a salad or simply with fresh basil 'Genovese', good olive oil and salt. Many houses in Italy have a food dryer (used mainly for drying porcini mushrooms) that can also be used to make sun-blushed (semi-dried) or sun-dried tomatoes.

Despite the fact that toms consist mainly of water, they are rich in vitamins, antioxidants and minerals, especially potassium and, with the exception of arthritis sufferers, whose symptoms can be aggravated by tomatoes, they are very beneficial. Red tomatoes contain about four times more beta-carotene than when green. While the flesh is very digestible, the skins can be quite tough, so skin them by dipping in boiling water and peeling before eating if you have any stomach or bowel disorders.

Spaghetti con Pomodori Ciliegini

SPAGHETTI WITH CHERRY TOMATOES

This typical Neapolitan dish uses cherry tomatoes of about 20–30 g. Any home-grown variety will be fine but I always use a hybrid variety called Lilliput F1. SERVES 2

500 g cherry tomatoes (Lilliput F1)
3 large cloves of garlic (Bianca Veneto), crushed
a pinch of fresh or dried oregano (Perenne Comune)
olive oil for frying
1 chilli pepper (Cayenna), deseeded and finely chopped

180 g thin spaghetti
30 g basil ('Genovese'), torn
3–4 tablespoons extra-virgin olive oil
salt and freshly ground black pepper
freshly grated Parmesan cheese

PREHEAT THE OVEN to Gas Mark 3/170°C. Cut the tomatoes in half and place on a baking tray. Sprinkle with the garlic, oregano and salt and pepper and bake for approximately 70 minutes, until semi-dry but still squashy. Heat a little oil in a large saucepan and lightly fry the chilli. Cook the spaghetti in boiling salted water until al dente. Drain and add to the saucepan. Stir in the tomatoes, basil, extra-virgin oil and ground pepper. To serve, sprinkle with freshly grated Parmesan cheese.

Pomodori Red Pear Franchi Ripieni

STUFFED RED PEAR FRANCHI TOMATOES

If you have planned when to eat this dish, pick the tomatoes a few days in advance and place with an apple in a dark drawer at room temperature, to really ripen off well. They'll go deep red and this process will really enhance their flavour. SERVES 4

4 large Red Pear Franchi tomatoes
200 g can tuna in olive oil
Italian mayonnaise
2 teaspoons capers

2 tablespoons flat-leaf parsley (Gigante di Napoli), chopped
salt and freshly ground black pepper

WASH THE TOMATOES, cut off the top third of each and leave to one side. Scoop out some of the flesh from inside the tomatoes to make a cavity, and put this aside also.

To make the filling, simply place the tuna, mayo to taste, capers, parsley and tomato flesh in a bowl and mix. Season to taste. Spoon this mixture into the tomatoes and place the tops back on at an angle so your guests can see the filling. Serve as an antipasto with prosciutto cotto (cooked ham) from your Italian deli.

CHILDHOOD BAKED STUFFED TOMATOES

by Jean-Christophe Novelli

This recipe conjures up many pleasant childhood memories. Beef tomatoes are definitely the best. Use large, firm but ripe tomatoes and, as soon as they are scooped, turn the tomatoes over to release the excess juice. Stuff, as here, with a savoury minced beef mixture and top with a little cheese. This dish was inspired by my mother. SERVES 4

4 beef tomatoes
4 tablespoons extra-virgin olive oil
2 teaspoons cumin seeds
100 g shallots or onions, diced
2 teaspoons caster sugar
1 tablespoon tomato purée
1 teaspoon Tabasco

4 sprigs thyme, stalks removed and chopped
10–12 basil leaves, torn
100 ml dry white wine
400 g lean minced beef
2 cloves of garlic, chopped
100 g cheese (Gruyère or Emmental), sliced
salt and freshly ground black pepper

PREHEAT THE OVEN to Gas Mark 3/170°C.

Cut a slice off the top of each tomato with a sharp knife and carefully remove the flesh. Take care not to cut through the skin. Reserve the shells and set aside.

Heat the flesh in a pan. Add a dash of olive oil and the cumin seeds. Bring to the boil, add the shallots or onions, sugar, tomato purée, Tabasco, thyme and half the basil and sweat gently for 3–5 minutes.

Pour in the white wine and stir in the beef. Reduce the heat, cover and cook for a further 5 minutes. Add the garlic and remaining basil leaves and stir to combine.

Season the tomato shells and place on a baking tray. Spoon in the beef and bake in the preheated oven for 10–12 minutes.

Remove from the oven, top with the cheese and return to the oven to bake for a further 5 minutes. Serve hot.

Linguine al Granchio

CRAB LINGUINE

Crab meat is very sweet and makes for super summer eating – children especially will love this dish. Use a fresh dressed crab from your fishmonger or even the excellent pasteurized crab meats you now see from Devon, but make sure there is both white and brown meat. Just, if at all possible, avoid canned crab meat: while canned white meat would be OK here, there will be no creamy dark meat to coat the linguine and give this dish its richness and substance – you would have to add cream to compensate. And don't use Cromer crabs – they are too good and should be enjoyed al naturale. SERVES 4

olive oil

2 large cloves of garlic (Rossa di Sulmona), thickly
    sliced

200 g cherry tomatoes (Red Cherry)

10 cm anchovy paste or 2 anchovies, chopped

½ glass white wine

500 g linguine

1 tablespoon tomato purée

120 g crab claws

a handful of parsley (Comune), chopped

120 g fresh dressed crab

butter

salt and freshly ground black pepper

chilli oil

HEAT A LARGE PAN OF WATER, ready to cook the pasta. Put a good slug of olive oil in a deep saucepan and add the garlic. Gently fry for just 1 minute before adding the cherry tomatoes and the anchovy paste or anchovies, as the garlic for this dish needs to be softened but still pale.

Cook for a couple of minutes or until the tomatoes start to open and their juices begin to run out. At this point, add a good slug of white wine, otherwise the tomato juice and the garlic could burn and go bitter.

Put the linguine on now as it will take about 7 minutes.

Add the tomato purée to the garlic and tomatoes and place the crab claws, along with any crab juices, in the pan now to warm through. Add the chopped parsley and cover.

When the pasta is ready and just before you drain it, add the dressed crab to the sauce with the remaining white wine and stir through. Taste the sauce for seasoning at this point and add a good pinch of salt and pepper, remembering that the anchovies are salty. Drain the linguine and place in the pan on top of the sauce and add 2 large knobs of butter.

Toss it all together so the linguine is coated evenly with the creamy crab dressing and serve straight away – without cheese, as this would mask the subtleness of the crab and make the dish too dry.

Allow each guest to add their own chilli oil at the table. Chilli oil added now (rather than adding chilli when cooking the sauce) will lift this type of dish. If everyone dresses their own plate with chilli oil, each guest can enjoy it as they like it. It's also a very Italian thing to do. Serve with scarpetta (bread – for mopping up) and a chilled Pinot Grigio.

Sugo di Pomodoro Freschi
FRESH TOMATO SAUCE by Mary Contini

The best cooking tomatoes come from Naples. This is a fact of life! Very soft, ripe San Marzano plum tomatoes cook down in no time, producing a full-flavoured, juicy, wonderful sugo. This sugo, served with spaghettini, encapsulates all I love about tomatoes – sweet, perfumed and delicate.

750 g ripe sweet tomatoes, preferably San Marzano, skinned
3–4 tablespoons extra-virgin olive oil
2 cloves of garlic, peeled
Maldon sea salt
a handful of fresh basil leaves, torn
360 g spaghettini
freshly ground black pepper

CUT THE TOMATOES INTO EVEN-SIZED PIECES. If you are lucky enough to find ripe, sweet, San Marzano plum tomatoes, then simply skin them and cut them into quarters lengthways.

Put the tomatoes into a large flat frying pan. Pour over the extra-virgin olive oil. Slice the garlic thinly on to the tomatoes. (This way the garlic cooks very gently and imparts a more delicate flavour than if cooked in oil first. The slivers are easily left on the plate when eating.) Cook the tomatoes over a low heat until they soften and collapse. Move them around from time to time; they'll take about 15 minutes. Add Maldon salt to bring out all the sweetness and flavour of the tomatoes. Check the seasoning. Stir the basil into the tomatoes.

Cook the pasta in boiling salted water and drain as soon as it is al dente. Give it a quick shake in the colander before tipping it into the tomato sugo. It will have a little of the cooking water clinging to it, which will just moisten the tomatoes enough. Warm it through and serve.

Tomato growing tips

There are two types of tomato – indeterminate (cordon) and determinate (bush). The former needs to have its 45-degree side shoots removed and the top shoot too, while the bush variety doesn't. There are more cordon varieties than bush, and the bush ones tend to be the smaller varieties, although in gardening there is always an exception.

The rules for growing a tomato are pretty much the same, whatever the variety. They'll grow in practically any soil, but prefer a rich, previously manured area if possible. You can of course grow tomatoes in growbags, which is great for a small garden or even the balcony of a flat. Remember though that growbags can dry out quickly so keep them well watered. They come with plant food in the compost, but this is used up quickly, so feed with a tomato feed in the summer after your tomato plants have developed two trusses (two sets of leaves). If growing in a growbag out in the garden, make a few cuts in the bottom of the bag so the roots can travel into the soil. Another benefit of growbags is that the compost is sterile; so if you have had problems with tomato blight or diseases in the soil, then use a growbag until your soil has been neutralized.

It's said by many that tomatoes that are 'stressed', or badly treated, will give the best-flavoured fruits, as they want to reproduce and so produce the best fruits to drop, which contain the seed for the next generation.

Always start tomatoes in pots or trays protected from the frost from January to the end of May. It is always best before you sow to fumigate your greenhouse and sterilize your equipment with, for example, Milton's and boiling water. Boiling water is also a very good and organic way to sterilize your soil, by the way. Don't forget to sterilize not only the containers and pots you sow into, but your tools and the canes that will support your toms. Clean the windows of your greenhouse as well, as the dirt could contain spores and disease.

You can acclimatize the plants before transplanting them out once there is no more risk of frost. Most cherry varieties, or pomodorini, can be grown from hanging baskets, although if you put them at the front of the house, expect a few to be nicked. Otherwise, plant out in a growbag or, better still, in garden soil in full sun. Feed them in the summer with a proprietary tomato feed. Slugs won't eat the plants, but other creatures might, so take the necessary precautions for your garden. You might have to spray the plants against diseases like tomato blight.

Tomato Principe Borghese da Appendere: This is the variety you get when you buy sun-dried tomatoes. Fruits of 90–100 g that are larger than a cherry tomato and smaller than a salad tom – about the size and shape of an egg. Indeterminate and a good cropper on the vine, these can be grown either inside or out. Ideal halved in salads or for drying, and excellent picked pink and hung in an airy, dark place for winter consumption.

Beef Tomato Costoluto Fiorentino: A regional variety found in Florence. Indeterminate, with semi-flat, misshapen and scalloped fruits – an heirloom variety with a superb flavour. Fruits of

150–180 g, preferably for growing under glass, but will grow outside in warmer parts of the UK, such as London, Devon and Cornwall. Excellent for eating raw in salads and for stuffing. An RHS Award of Garden Merit winner.

Semi Plum Tomato Roma: Well known both in the UK and the USA, where it is sometimes referred to as a 'paste' tomato. Juicy enough to eat and meaty enough for cooking, but best of all it's a determinate variety that will grow outside. Fruits typically of 70–80g. Ideal for eating fresh, for freezing (for later use in cooking), and for making sauces, soups and passata.

Plum Tomato San Marzano: Possibly the worst eating tomato on the planet! But because they are very dry and meaty, with thin skin and very few seeds, they are one of the best cooking tomatoes in the world, if not the best. Indeterminate with fruits of 70–80 g that can be grown outside. Suitable for freezing whole, cutting raw for pizza toppings, for making tomato sauces, soups and passata, and for all dishes using cooked tomatoes.

Beef Tomato Beefmaster F1: A very large hybrid beef tomato with fruits that can grow over 500 g in weight each. If you threw this at someone, you'd kill them. Indeterminate, with slightly green shoulders, which some people like and some don't (I do). This one really needs to be grown under glass in the UK and is ideal for slicing into salads, eating with olive oil or for stuffing.

Cherry Tomato Lilliput F1: Cherry tomatoes are called 'pomodorini' in Italy and are often sold still on the vine. They can be grown in pots, or even hanging baskets, outside, and are a determinate variety with fruits slightly larger than a large cherry (about 20–30 g each). They are productive and very sweet and are best bitten into with the mouth closed!

Plum Tomato San Marzano Redorta: Truncheon-sized giant plum tomatoes from Bergamo, which are surprisingly juicy and, so, versatile enough to eat raw or cooked, or used for sauces and passata. An indeterminate variety, it has fruits of about 350 g and is best grown indoors.

Yellow Salad Tomato Tondo Giallo Golden Boy: Yellow tomatoes are quite old-fashioned. They are nice and sweet and add colour to the salad bowl. This is an F1 hybrid and an indeterminate variety. Its fruits are 140–160 g and are really intended for the salad bowl, although they look attractive when sliced and cooked on to pizzas.

Beef Tomato Red Pear Franchi: A really Italian tomato in the shape of a lightly scalloped fat pear. Cut it in half and it's all meat – very few seeds and, although juicy, not a wet tom. It is ideal for stuffing because of both its robustness and shape. It is an indeterminate tomato with fruits weighing about 220–230 g and is usually always picked completely green, or just turning pink, and stored.

Tomato Big Rio 2000 F1: Mid/early semi plum tomato. Determinate variety that can be used either for sauces or for eating fresh.

Tomato San Marzano Astro F1: There are a lot of different types of San Marzano tomatoes and this is sometimes called the San Marzano Nano or dwarf San Marzano, as it's a bush variety. You sometimes see this type of tomato growing on the ground with no support at all in large fields in the south of Italy. It is mainly a cooking tomato and is resistant to rot and also verticillium and fusarium (two diseases that tomatoes can get). It is an excellent producer of oblong tomatoes.

Tomato San Marzano Follia: Follia (madness!) looks pretty similar to Astro except for a little nipple at the end whereas Astro has a rounded end. But it is quite different in that it is an indeterminate variety and it is recommended for eating fresh rather than cooking, which is unusual for a San Marzano tomato. It has thick flesh, is productive and also resistant to some disease. A really good tomato and a favourite in our garden at home.

Tomato Yellow Pear Shaped: An early variety producing small, yellow, tear-drop cherry tomatoes that are both very attractive and most unusual. Vigorous producer of sweet fruits and can be grown either indoors or out. Indeterminate.

Pachino Cherry Tomatoes: These tomatoes are found only in Sicily. They have an IGP rating (Indicazione Geografica Protetta), which is similar to a DOC or DOCG on a wine. It guarantees the area of production. The most common are indeterminate with fruits of 20–30 g each, but any tomato variety grown in the Pachino zone is a pachino tomato – there is no one variety known as 'Pachino'.

lattuga

e altre foglie di insalata

LETTUCE AND OTHER SALAD LEAVES

Generally speaking, lettuces are mainly used for salads, but there are some great varieties in Italy that are often cooked, especially from the endive and escarole family, as well as radicchios.

All leaves such as endives and chicories are beneficial, and lettuces are no exception. They contain good levels of chlorophyll, vitamins and mineral salts and, because they are generally eaten raw, none of those vitamins are lost in cooking. Lettuces can be hard to digest: as a sufferer of Crohn's disease, I have to avoid them when I am having an attack.

You need to spend extra time cleaning lettuces, as they can carry listeria or toxoplasmosis and other bacteria associated with the earth. Pregnant women should take special care.

SALAD OF PRAWNS with 'Lattuga' Sauce, Basil and Orange Segments

by Chef Maurizio Morelli, Latium, London

SERVES 4

20 large uncooked prawns
2 heads of lettuce (Regina dei Ghiacci)
extra-virgin olive oil
2 oranges

1 clove of garlic, finely sliced
8 basil leaves
salt and freshly ground black pepper

CLEAN THE PRAWNS FROM THEIR SHELLS, removing the heads, and put aside.

Wash the lettuce leaves and cook half of them in boiling salted water for 5 minutes. Strain the lettuce from the water and place in a blender with 1 tablespoon extra-virgin olive oil. Blend to create a smooth sauce.

Peel the oranges, divide into deseeded segments and mix with the remaining lettuce leaves. Season to taste with salt and pepper and dress with some olive oil.

Heat a frying pan with olive oil, add the prawns and garlic and cook for 2 minutes each side. Season with salt and pepper.

Spoon the lettuce sauce on to a plate, covering the whole base, and place the cooked prawns around the edge. Place the lettuce and orange salad in the middle. Now take the fresh basil leaves, tear them and sprinkle all over the salad.

Serve with a bottle of chilled Italian white wine.

'Nei campi *si vive*, in casa si muore'

IN THE FIELDS YOU LIVE AND IN THE HOUSE YOU DIE

Insalata Misticanza

MIXED LEAF SALAD

You could add fresh onion, fennel, radish, tomato or cucumber to this salad, or use it as a base for Salade Niçoise, adding black olives, hard-boiled eggs, croûtons and anchovies.

mixed leaves (lettuce, chicory, radicchio, endive, escarole, lamb's lettuce, etc.)
olive oil
red wine vinegar or lemon juice
salt and freshly ground black pepper

WASH THE SALAD LEAVES and dry properly. This will ensure the dressing coats the leaves effectively. Dress with a vinaigrette made with olive oil, vinegar or lemon, salt and pepper.

CAESAR SALAD

This is an Italian-inspired dish from America, created by a man called Cardini. It has become rather commercialized and a bit 1980s, but if you make it yourself it really is a very nice rediscovery. It can be enjoyed as an accompaniment to meats but is hearty enough as a meal in its own right! I find that Caesar salad is best served as a complete dish rather than a side, so if you want to serve meat with it, place a couple of grilled chicken breasts on top (don't mix them into the salad).

If you prefer, buy a ready-made Caesar dressing, but do try and use your own home-grown Romaine lettuces. SERVES 2 AS A MAIN COURSE

1 clove of garlic, grated	*salt and freshly ground black pepper*
100 ml extra-virgin olive oil	For the dressing
100 g stale bread, cubed, for croûtons	*1 egg (see method)*
1 Romaine lettuce (Romana), washed and torn up	*2–3 anchovy fillets, chopped*
Worcestershire sauce	*juice of ½ lemon*
50 g Parmesan or Pecorino cheese, grated	*1 clove of garlic, grated*

PREHEAT THE OVEN to Gas Mark 4/180°C.

Add 1 grated garlic clove to half the olive oil. Pour this oil on to the cubed bread until absorbed, place on a baking tray and bake in the oven for about 15 minutes, or until browned. Remove and allow to cool.

It is important to use a very fresh egg for the dressing as it will, in essence, be raw. If it is not already at room temperature, place it in a glass of water for 10 minutes. Then 'coddle' the egg by putting it into a cup and pouring boiling water over it, leaving it for no more than 1 minute before removing and running under cold water. This process thickens the yolk and makes the dressing even richer. Separate the yolk from the white.

Mix the dressing ingredients together, adding the egg yolk last.

Place the lettuce in a salad bowl and add the remaining oil, Worcestershire sauce to taste, the grated cheese, and the Caesar dressing, mixing well to ensure the leaves are evenly coated. Season to taste. Sprinkle the croûtons over the salad.

Lettuce growing tips

Lettuces can have a very long sowing season and you can harvest them until the first hard frosts outside. They can be sown 1 cm down pretty much from February until the end of September/October, depending on the variety, and there is even one called Meraviglia d'Inverno San Martino which can be sown protected until the end of December. You can also extend their season by growing in a polytunnel or greenhouse. There are many, many different types, shapes and colours and they are generally not bothered about specific soil types or feeding.

Slugs and snails like lettuce so you may have to use slug pellets, beer traps or other measures. I don't much care for slug pellets, but I do use them, sparingly, from time to time when it has been very wet. Beer traps work well, as do coffee beans, as they release emollient oils that the slugs don't like, but the best I have found so far is Marmite. If you smear it around your pots or containers, slugs will not cross it because it is so salty, and you know what salt does to slugs and snails.

There are two main groups of lettuce: cutting lettuces and lettuce heads.

CUTTING LETTUCES These are found in green or red varieties and offer convenience and growing ease. They can be grown in pots if desired. They grow quicker than a head of lettuce, you cut as much as you need and they grow back again after cutting. If you only need two leaves for a sandwich, then just cut two leaves; with a head of lettuce you need to take the whole head. These types of lettuces are often called 'cut and come again', but it's not worth cutting them more than three times as the leaves can start to go hard.

Some varieties worth seeking out are: Green – Green Salad Bowl, Bionda Ricciolina, Verde Ricciolina, Bionda a Foglia di Quercia and Bionda a Foglia Liscia; Red – Rossa Ricciolina, Mora d'Inverno, Biscia Rossa and Red Salad Bowl.

LETTUCE HEADS Self-explanatory, but there really are a large range of lettuce heads, ranging from upright (Romaine) to closed (Iceberg) to open (butterhead).

Romaine lettuces are the ones used mainly for making Caesar Salads; the name is a bastardization of the word 'Romana' or Roman. They are crunchy and really tasty. Surprisingly, there are many different varieties of Romaine – Bionda degli Ortolani, Verde degli Ortolani, delle 7 Lune, Mortarella, Lentissima, Lentissima sel. Franchi and Bougival, to name a few. The classic one is Bionda degli Ortolani but try the 7 Lune, which is covered with delightful red splodges. Romaine lettuces have a tendency to bolt with heat, and it's recommended you avoid sowing them in June and July.

Iceberg types are crisp lettuces that shred really well – the classic deli lettuce. They should taste good, as long as you can find an outlet that sells ones with a home-grown flavour and not the mass-produced tasteless green bowling balls that go so well with the ready meals they sell of the same quality.

Finally there are the open-headed, soft-leaf varieties like the butterhead Testa di Burro, S. Anna, Trionfo d'Estate and the purple/red Quattro Stagioni, and the ruffled lettuces, the kings of which are the well-known Lollo verde (green) and Lollo Rossa (red), but the green Gentillina is also very good and resists summer heat. The red lettuces add colour to your salad bowl, but salads are best when mixed leaves are used.

Here are some of the main varieties, regional and national, and their characteristics.

Misticanza: This simply means 'mixture' and is usually a selection of different leaves – red ones, green ones, crinkly and straight, soft and crunchy. A whole salad in one packet that should be sown in succession from April to September to ensure a continuous harvest. I am writing this in January and I still have an unheated greenhouse full of these leaves.

Batavia Bionda Bordo Rosso: A late green lettuce with red lacing on frilly edges. The head is round, crispy and a good variety for market.

Batavia Bionda di Parigi: A late lettuce from Paris with a large, tightly wrapped head. Light green tender leaves with pronounced, slightly frilly, crunchy ribs. Harvest until November.

Maravilla de Verano Canasta: A Spanish variety grown widely in Italy. Mid/late, green with scarlet edging and a good-sized head. A very nice lettuce. Sow from February to mid September.

Regina delle Ghiacciole: 'Queen of the Ice' or, as we call 'em in English, Iceberg lettuces. They can be mass-produced and tasteless, but home-grown Icebergs tend to have more flavour (surprise, surprise) and they are the ideal shredding lettuce. Late. Sow from mid February to end of August.

Rossa di Trento: Trento is in the Dolomites, very alpine and a very cold region of Italy. Rossa di Trento should be sown from March to mid September and can be harvested until mid November. It's a cracker, with a large head, big green leaves blushed with red, flavour and crispness second to none.

Sant'Anna: Saint Anna is the patron saint of pregnant women Her feast day is 26 July, and this lettuce is sown only from March to 26 July. It is a butterhead type, but with a more closed head, and is resistant to summer heat.

Biscia Rossa: Literally, 'Red Snake'. An early lettuce, open-headed, green and red with ruffled leaves and quite rustic. Sow from February to April and July to August.

Red Salad Bowl: An early, reliable and very popular lettuce which is 'cut and come again'. Easy to grow. Sow from February to October. Grows quickly and adds colour to the salad bowl.

Mora d'Inverno: 'Winter Brunette', a rustic variety. Early with an open splaying head and blistered leaves. Sow March to May and July to August and harvest until the end of November.

Regina di Maggio: 'May Queen'. An early, round green lettuce with a closed head that is not tightly wrapped. Sow from March to May and July to August.

Gentillina: A mid/early variety that is slow to bolt. It has lovely frilly leaves, an open habit and a good-sized head. Sow from February to the end of September.

Lollo Bionda: Early. Lollo is a very well-known lettuce that is available in most supermarkets. These probably don't come from Italy, whereas if you grow them from Italian seed, you know you're getting the real thing. Large, frilly heads and a very long sowing season from February right until the end of October. Why wouldn't you eat this lettuce all year?

Lollo Rossa: Even more famous than its green cousin. Red, ruffled leaves and, like the green lollo, you can harvest it until the end of November. Always wash shop-bought lollo lettuces well because they can be quite sandy.

Testa di Burro: 'Winter Butterhead'. An early variety that is recommended for an autumn/winter harvest. The head is slighty closed but not tightly wrapped and it has soft melt-in-the-mouth leaves. Sow from March to May and July to September, avoiding summer heat. Harvest right up until November.

Romaine Bionda degli Ortolani: A Romaine lettuce, upright and very crunchy with a super flavour. Mid/early and a classic for Caesar salads. Sow from March to September.

Romaine delle 7 Lune: 'Romaine of the 7 Moons'. A rustic variety that is green but covered in red splodges like paint splats. Sow from March to September, avoiding June.

Romaine Mortarella: Mid/early variety with a head of medium dimensions, upright and compact. The leaves are intense green with a slight red smoking around the edges.

Romaine Lentissima sel. Franchi F1: A superior Franchi variety Romaine lettuce that is very slow to bolt. Upright, tightly wrapped head with good texture. Crunchy and consistent with good flavour. Sow from February to May and July to September.

Romaine Bougival: Mid/early Romaine lettuce. A rustic variety of good dimensions. Upright, with tightly wrapped green leaves. Crunchy with very pronounced ribs and a rustic variety.

Lettuce Pesciatina: Mid/early. Round closed head with green and red edging, dimpled, tender, crunchy. Sow from March to September.

Passion Brune: A stunning late, green variety stained with deep red and with good resistance to cold. It can be harvested until the end of December. Vigorous plant with a round, well-proportioned head. Produces crisp green blistered leaves with red lacing.

Quattro Stagioni: 'Four Seasons'. A mid/early lettuce with beautiful scarlet-red staining and a closed head that is green inside. Sow from March to end of September.

Bionda Ricciolina: Very early, this cutting lettuce produces beautiful soft lime-green leaves, held up by a crunchy rib at the back. The leaves are ruffled and can be sown from mid February to end of September. 'Cut and come again' variety.

Rossa Ricciolina: Very similar characteristics to Bionda Ricciolina, except in red! If you grow both together, you will have a real mixed salad. Red ruffled leaves, which in general become more red the cooler it is. Slow to bolt.

Bionda a Foglia Liscia: Very early cutting lettuce. Sow from March all the way to end of October. It grows very quickly and has a small, lamb's-tongue-shaped rounded leaf that will grow back after cutting.

Unicum: Similar to an Iceberg lettuce, Unicum is mid/late with a large, round head, crunchy and slow to bolt. Sow from March to end of July and harvest until the end of October.

Meraviglia d'Inverno San Martino: Winter variety. Compact, tender open head with ruffled green leaves, a variety that resists cold. You can sow it in a cold greenhouse from July to December and harvest September to end of March! Sow February to December. A must-have for winter.

Great Lakes: Large green head with large, crunchy and numerous leaves. Sow from March to June.

Ubriacona: A large-headed lettuce, called 'Drunkard' because of its red-flushed cheeks. Sow from March to end of September.

Ciucca: Mid/early variety with round, semi-open head of good dimensions. The ample leaves are blistered, tender and crunchy and an intense green colour with red smoking. Sow from January to end of March and again from September to October as it doesn't like the heat. In the UK harvest until about the end of December.

Parella Rossa/Rougette de Montpelier: Open head of compact dimensions. Good resistance to low temperatures, even sub-zero. Sow from February to April and from September to October and harvest April to June and November to December.

Parella Verde: Mid-sized open head with fat leaves and black seeds. Sow from February to April and from September to October. Harvest up to the end of December and sometimes into January.

Rouge Grenobloise: French alpine lettuce from Grenoble. Mid/late with semi-open head. Green leaves with deep red borders. Sow from February to September and harvest until the end of November.

Endives and Escaroles The experts on these are the French and the Italians, although the Americans make use of them infinitely more than the British.

In the UK we tend to think of endives as the French 'frisée' type, wonderful, slightly bitter with tough, serrated leaves and large splaying heads. These are always used in a salad, especially later on in the season and have beautiful blanched yellow hearts, turning greener towards the outer leaves.

But the real gem, and I think the best-kept Franco-Italian secret, is the escarole, as it's known in France and America, or scarola as it's called in Italy. Very large open heads with leaves so crunchy, they almost shatter in the mouth when bitten into. If you bend the leaves, they snap, rather than break. There's hardly any bitterness and this is a variety that is cooked as often as it's eaten raw. In the US, virtually every Italian restaurant has escarole on the menu. It's almost always sautéed in olive oil with garlic and served hot as a vegetable, and it is very good. We're not talking about wacky lettuce soups or other weird concoctions. This variety cooks really, really well.

Zuppa di Scarola
ESCAROLE SOUP

This recipe is from Bill McKay, who is one of the Franchi agents in America. His mother was from the Abruzzo region of Italy, and this is a variation on how she used to make it. There are as many ways of making escarole soup as there are cooks in Italy.

A variation on the bread is to add some cooked cannellini beans or broken pieces of pasta about 15 minutes before the end of cooking. SERVES 4

1 clove of garlic, plus more to serve	*1.2 litres stock or water*
1 small onion, chopped	*2 tomatoes, roughly chopped*
50–75 g pancetta, chopped	*1 head of escarole, cleaned and chopped into*
olive oil	*bite-sized pieces*
2–3 celery sticks, chopped	*bread slices*

COOK THE GARLIC, ONION AND PANCETTA in some olive oil. Don't let things brown. Add the celery, followed by the stock and the tomatoes. Bring to the boil and simmer for 15–20 minutes. Add the escarole and continue cooking until everything is done.

To serve, grill or toast some slices of good bread. Rub with garlic, place in a soup bowl and ladle the soup over the grilled bread.

Endive and Escarole growing tips

They can be sown from June to end of September and harvested outside until the end of December, although they will usually overwinter in our mild UK climate. Don't be tempted to sow them in the spring along with your other lettuces, you won't get very good results. It's an endive, not a lettuce, even if it looks more like a lettuce. They need heat initially to germinate and start their journey, and then cold to develop. Most varieties are very hardy and will tolerate sub-zero.

There are several varieties of escarole and endive; the open-headed ones should be tied up about seven to ten days before harvest to blanch the heart and make them tender. Or you can just stick a bucket on top and, when you harvest that head, move the bucket to the next one. Be lazy – use an elastic band. Be even lazier and plant them closer than the standard 20 cm apart, so they all bunch up and blanch themselves.

Scarola Verde a Cuor Pieno: Classic escarole. This is one of the better cooking varieties, in my opinion, and has a large head with a golden heart that melts in the mouth. The most widely known scarola in Italy.

Bionda a Cuor Pieno: One of the best for eating in salads as it has a large, blonde heart and is therefore very tender.

Bordeaux: The benefit of this French variety is that it grows upright, like a Romaine lettuce. This means that it is self-blanching.

Bubykopf: Mid/early and similar to the Scarola Verde in characteristics and appearance, except that Bubykopf is more compact. Also excellent for cooking.

Gigante di Bergamo: A regional variety from Bergamo with a very large splaying head. Mid/late, it has excellent resistance to cold and can usually be harvested until the end of December.

Endive Pancalieri: Pancalieri is near Turin. This is a classic 'frisée' type of endive with serrated, tough leaves. They have a pleasant bitterness about them, which is tempered by using a nice sweet balsamic vinegar. Sow from June onwards and harvest with the cold.

Endive Cuor d'Oro: Similar to Pancalieri but with a tighter head and a larger golden heart once blanched. Sow from June to end of August and harvest until the end of December.

Endive Romanesco da Taglio: Roman cutting endive with thin, jagged upright leaves that grow in small bunches. This is a very easy variety to grow and use and it has a long sowing season. Sow from April to October and harvest May to mid December.

Radicchio and Chicory In the UK we tend to think of chicories as the green-leafed varieties and radicchios as the types with red leaves, although both are from the chicory family and both share a similar pleasant bitter taste that adds so much to a humble salad – a different texture, flavour, crunchiness. Italians love bitter flavours, from China Martini and Campari to Chinotto (Italian Coke!) and our beloved chicories.

Sometimes people comment that their home-grown chicory and radicchio is too bitter. This is easily remedied. A trick used by my aunt in Venice is to add a teaspoon of sugar or honey to the dressing. This doesn't make the dressing sweeter, it simply counterbalances the bitterness of the chicory. Another tip is to soak the leaves for 30 minutes in cold, salted water, which will extract some of the bitter properties. Be sure to rinse them before serving. You could also grow a cutting chicory, which will always be milder than one that forms a head.

All chicories can be added to a salad and, besides providing different textures and flavours, they have beneficial properties – aiding digestion and containing mineral salts and vitamins. Radicchios, in addition to being eaten fresh like green chicories, can be cooked and make a delicious vegetable. A Treviso or Palla Rossa (red ball) chicory, for example, can be cut up and pan-fried in a little olive oil, or brushed with olive oil and salt and barbecued. The flavour changes when cooked, becoming sweet and caramelly, with a pleasant bitter aftertaste that is really pleasing on the palate.

Insalata di Radicchio e Pere
SALAD OF RADICCHIO, Pear, Chestnuts and Gorgonzola by Gennaro Contaldo

The bitter-tasting radicchio goes really well with the sweet pears and, to give the salad a bit of body, I have added some chestnuts and Gorgonzola cheese. Leave these out, if you prefer, and simply enjoy the radicchio and pears. SERVES 4

2 pears, cored and cut into thin slices, then placed in lemon juice to avoid discoloration
2 heads of radicchio, leaves removed
200 g peeled roasted chestnuts, cut into quarters
120 g Gorgonzola cheese, cut into cubes
a few chopped chive stalks to garnish

For the dressing
1 shallot, finely chopped
1 teaspoon English mustard
2 tablespoons cider vinegar
120 ml extra-virgin olive oil
salt and freshly ground black pepper

MAKE THE DRESSING by mixing all the ingredients together.

Place the rest of the ingredients except the chives in a large bowl. Pour over the dressing and toss well. Garnish with the chives.

Radicchio Rossa di Treviso in Frittura

BREADCRUMBED RADICCHIO ROSSA DI TREVISO

Radicchio is eaten mainly in the north-west of Italy, especially in the Veneto region. We are often unadventurous about cooking salad leaves, but radicchio of Treviso is one where it works really well. If it's not available you could also use the Palla Rossa type, which has tightly wrapped heads. The name translates literally as 'red ball'. SERVES 4

4 heads of radicchio (Rossa di Treviso)

4 tablespoons flour mixed with a pinch of salt

2 small eggs, beaten

breadcrumbs for coating

olive oil

CLEAN THE RADICCHIO and remove some of the outer leaves. Cut the remaining central part into quarters. Dry each piece and coat in flour, followed by the beaten egg and then the breadcrumbs. Fry in olive oil until golden brown. Remove from the oil and place on kitchen paper for a minute before arranging on plates for serving.

GRILLED RADICCHIO WITH MELTED CHEESE
by Hugh Fearnley-Whittingstall

The harsh, bitter taste of radicchio, Treviso and other red chicories is not everybody's cup of tea and, to be honest, it's not always mine. But I grow them in my polytunnel anyway because, for the money, these hardy winter salad plants come into their own when thoughts of salad are banished and they are cooked for a change. The bitterness is mollified and their natural sweetness comes to the fore. A trickle of olive oil and a generous slab of melting cheese dissipate the last traces of austerity and make this a gluttonous winter treat. Incidentally, this dish also works well with sweeter summer lettuces such as Little Gem. SERVES 4 AS A STARTER

CUT 4 TIGHT HEADS OF TREVISO or other radicchio into quarters, leaving the base of the stems intact to hold the leaves together. Brush them with olive oil and season well with salt and pepper.

Then place cut-side down on a preheated heavy griddle pan – preferably the kind with raised ridges. Cook for 3–5 minutes, turning occasionally. They are ready when the outer leaves are well charred and striped from the grill and the stems are just becoming tender.

Arrange the quarters in a dish and lay thin slices of your chosen cheese over them: it might be goat's cheese or Taleggio (a personal favourite) or torta di dolcelatte. Add a few more twists of pepper and another trickle of olive oil and place in a very hot oven, or under a grill, until the cheese starts to bubble. Serve at once, four quarters per person.

Risotto con Radicchio e Luganica
RISOTTO WITH RADICCHIO AND ITALIAN SAUSAGE

SERVES 4

1 small white onion (Musona), sliced
olive oil
3 Italian luganica sausages, sliced
350–400 g arborio, carnaroli or Sant' Andrea
*   risotto rice*
½ glass white wine

1 litre chicken stock
1–2 heads of radicchio (Rossa di Treviso or
*   Verona), roughly chopped*
salt and freshly ground black pepper
butter, to serve
freshly grated Parmesan, to serve

USING A LARGE, HEAVY FRYING PAN, soften the onion in a little olive oil. Place the sausage slices in the pan and fry until slightly browned. Add the rice together with the white wine and then, after 1–2 minutes, enough stock to just cover the rice. Risotto rice takes about 20 minutes to cook depending on the variety and you will need to keep adding the stock a spoonful at a time so that it doesn't dry out. Risotto should be slightly fluid, but not liquid when served.

After about 10 minutes, add the radicchio and season to taste. Stir occasionally, especially towards the end of cooking, as it can stick. Test the risotto before serving to make sure the rice is cooked through.

When ready to serve, add a knob of butter to glaze the risotto, and serve with freshly grated Parmesan and a glass of good red wine (Gattinara, Spanna, Barolo or Amarone).

DANDELION AND BACON SALAD by Jimmy Doherty ('Jimmy's Farm')

These little beauties grow everywhere, even on the scraggiest bit of ground. Mixed with bacon they make a wicked salad, so get out there, start picking and start enjoying! SERVES 2 AS A STARTER

115 g dry-cured streaky bacon, diced
170 g young dandelion leaves, washed
sea salt and freshly ground black pepper

3 tablespoons olive oil or bacon fat
1 tablespoon white wine vinegar

FRY THE BACON until crisp and dry. Put the dandelion leaves in a bowl and season with salt and pepper. Turn them gently in the oil or fat and vinegar. Tip in the bacon and mix again gently.

You could make this more substantial by topping it with a soft-poached egg or maybe some soft-boiled quails' eggs.

Radicchio and Chicory growing tips

There's quite a difference between the two types. Chicories (the green ones), are treated much like lettuces in that they have the same growing season and are not generally frost hardy (sow from February to September/October). These are best eaten raw in salads.

Radicchios are generally from the alpine northern part of Italy and are completely hardy. They are generally sown much later and harvested through the winter. In fact, many radicchio varieties actually need the cold to turn red. Some varieties can withstand temperatures of -15°C and can be harvested outside in the UK from November to April.

Cold is what makes radicchio turn red, and herein lies the problem. If you buy seed and sow it in March, April or May you end up with a big green head like a Romaine lettuce, which turns hairy and so bitter that it is inedible. The reason for this is that it's being planted with cold and grown into heat, when in reality you need to sow it with heat (around the end of August) and grow it into the cold. I always plant mine when I come back from my summer holidays and the plant will look green, but then, come October, you see a slight red tinge and by November, December, the radicchio turns red. The colder it is, the redder – and sweeter – radicchio is. This is why you don't see radicchio of Sicily or Naples, but of Verona, Treviso, Bergamo and Milano.

Some chicories are variegated and look brilliant. The most striking of these are Variegata di Castelfranco and Romea or Fladige. As these are sometimes in the middle in terms of colour, people are often unsure whether to call them chicories or radicchios. The best chicories for the salad bowl are the Pan di Zucchero (head), Bianca di Milano (head), Grumolo Bionda (blonde rosettes for cutting), Grumolo Verde (green rosettes), Zuccherina di Trieste (cutting), da Taglio a Foglia Larga (large-leafed, cutting), Bianca di Chioggia (head), Mantovana (head) and Spadona (cutting). Then there are the Catalogna chicories, which look like big, sturdy upright dandelions. These can be eaten raw, but in some regions of Italy they cook them and use them as a sauce with garlic, onion, salt and olive oil. The main varieties are from Puglia and Brindisi, where it can still get cold, although there are also two varieties from the Veneto region.

The best-known radicchio is the Rossa di Treviso, which is the red and white striped upright variety often found in salad packs. They look awful, but just throw away the straggly outer leaves and you are left with your prize. This is the best variety for cooking.

Both green and red chicories are sown at 1 cm depth; green chicories from March onwards and sometimes until October, red chicories (radicchios) from June to September onwards. See sowing details for each variety. There is one chicory that is not Italian but is used all over Europe. This is the Belgian witloof-style chicory, which is yellow. The plant is grown and then the leaves are cut back and the roots are carefully lifted from the soil and placed into a bucket of sand or a cool dark room for the sweet yellow 'chicons' to form.

There is a problem with identifying chicory (and other vegetable) varieties because all over Italy the same variety may have a different name, depending on where you are. For example, Selvatica da Campo, or wild chicory, is called Gruniag in Piacenza and Erba Cucca in Piedmont.

Radicchio Rossa di Treviso: Upright red and white striped variety from north-west Italy that turns red and sweeter with the cold. Can be eaten raw or cooked. Discard the outer leaves. Sow from June to August and harvest until the end of December.

Radicchio Rossa di Treviso Svelta: Commonly referred to as 'Black of Treviso', owing to its deep purple colour. Svelta is the earliest of the Trevisos and the word means 'quickly'. Harvest until the end of November.

Radicchio Rossa di Treviso Tardiva: This is the latest of the Treviso-type radicchios. It easily resists frosts and can be harvested as late as the end of March. Compact and tight, with a long head and thin, meaty, curved leaves.

Variegated Radicchio of Lusia Tardiva: Large late variety with ample leaves. Green with red specks. Tasty and crunchy. Good resistance to frosts. Sow from June/July to end of September. Harvest October to end of February.

Chicory Pan di Zucchero: 'Sugerloaf'. Upright green variety with long tight head. Used widely. An ideal variety for shredding. RHS Award of Garden Merit winner. Sow from June to August.

Chicory Bianca di Milano: Upright green chicory with tightly packed, large head. Sow from June to August and harvest October to mid December.

Chicory Grumolo Bionda: Open rosette-shaped leaves. Sow from mid March to the end of October and harvest from May the same year to February the following year.

Chicory Zuccherina di Trieste: 'Sugar of Trieste'. Very early. Tender leaves that grow easily and that are 'cut and come again'. Sow from March to end of September.

Radicchio Palla Rossa di Verona: A classic 'red ball' variety, late and very hardy with thick white ribs. Sow from June to end of August and harvest until the end of March. Like all radicchios, they won't turn red unless subjected to low temperatures.

Radicchio Palla Rossa Precoce: Mid/early. 'Red ball'-type chicory that is not winter hardy and is therefore harvested until about mid November. Tightly wrapped head with white veining.

Radicchio Palla Rossa 6 Agena: Late. A large head with sweeping white veining and a compact head. Resistant to low temperatures, so can be harvested from December to end of January.

Radicchio Palla Rossa 6 Marzatica: A late, sturdy and productive plant. It will produce robust outer leaves with internal leaves of deep red with white veining. Resistant to very low temperatures and can be harvested until the end of March.

Variegated Palla Rossa of Chioggia: Mid/early with red and white mottled leaves and round closed head. From the Veneto region of Italy. Sow from June to end of August and harvest until the end of November.

Radicchio Palla Rossa Pagoda: A late variety that is resistant to low temperatures. The veining is consistent and looks like lightning on the red leaves. Sow from mid July to end of August and harvest until end of January.

Radicchio Rossa di Verona sel. Arca: Head of fair dimensions with large crunchy ribs and no veining. Early. Sow from July to August and harvest until mid February.

Chicory Bianca di Chioggia: From the Veneto region, this mid/late chicory forms a round green head with red-veined edges. Unusually for a green chicory, it is resistant to low temperatures and hence harvested until mid February.

Puntarelle Catalogna Chicory di Galatina: Early. Upright chicory with serrated leaves and pine-cone-shaped buds at the base. You grow this variety precisely for the 'puntarelle' buds, which are sliced and dressed with olive oil and fresh lemon juice.

Radicchio Orchidea Rossa: 'Red Orchid'. Looks like a large red flower head, hence its beautiful name. Sow in March and again from June to September.

Variegated Chicory of Castelfranco: This chicory has two crops: first it will give you an open yellow head of chicory that looks as if it has been splattered with red paint, then you can pull the roots and produce sweet yellow 'chicons' by putting them in sand and depriving them of light.

Yellow Chicory Witloof: This variety is Belgian and is primarily used to produce the yellow 'chicons' that are so popular in Belgium. Cut back the foliage and gently lift the roots. Store in a crate of sand or soil mixed with sand. Commercially, they are brought on in cool, dark rooms.

Chicory da Radice di Soncino: An unusual chicory whose white, carrot-like root is harvested much like a dandelion root. Can be eaten raw, cooked or made into chicory coffee. Sow from April to the end of July.

Chicory Spadona: Early cutting variety with lance-shaped single leaves. Because they are long, they bunch well and so are particularly suited for market. Sow from March to September.

Radicchio Grumolo Rossa: Late red radicchio that you 'cut and come again'. Forms the beautiful characteristic rosette-shaped heads in late season with the cold. Sow from May to September and harvest from October to March.

Chicory Selvatica da Campo: Wild chicory, which resembles spindly dandelion leaves and is eaten from central Italy to the north. Sow from May to the end of August.

Dandelion Dente di Leone: In France, known as 'pis en lit' (wet the bed) because of their diuretic properties. If cultivating, blanch them to make sure they are tender and sweet enough. Every part of the dandelion can be eaten, from the flowers to the roots.

Other Leaves Mixing lettuce leaves with other leaves adds different textures, colours and flavours to your salads. Lamb's lettuce, sometimes called lamb's tongue because of the shape of the leaves, is known as mâche in France (sometimes in the UK too) and corn salad in the US. It has the most velvety soft leaves and melt-in-the-mouth texture.

Rocket is as popular now as it was in Roman times owing to its wonderfully strong and peppery flavour. You can throw it into a salad or a sandwich (try prawns or roast beef with rocket), it goes well with strong cheeses like Roquefort or dolcelatte, in frittata (Italian omelettes), on bruschetta and on the classic pizza 'Rucola e Bresaola' (rocket and cured fillet of beef). If you like pesto, try using rocket instead of basil. This makes a good dip and an even better pasta sauce. But be careful, as there are two types of rocket, cultivated and wild, and one is stronger than the other, so adjust your recipes accordingly. Wild rocket is too strong to use for making rocket pesto, but is great placed raw on top of a cooked pizza, as it will wilt and warm through.

Bistecca con Gorgonzola e Ruccola alla Guiseppina
GIUSEPPINA'S STEAK WITH GORGONZOLA AND ROCKET

Giuseppina Castagna runs the Genzianella bar in our village, Villa del Bosco (villa in the woods), in Piedmont. Anyway, one of my favourite dishes was Giuseppina Castagna's steak topped with Gorgonzola, a cheese local to our area. The steak would be medium rare and the Gorgonzola would be drizzling down the sides, almost making a sauce. Italian Gorgonzola is mild and very creamy; often the Gorgonzola available in the UK is very strong and firm. This type of mountain Gorgonzola will overpower and kill the steak, so select your cheese at a speciality cheese shop or your Italian deli, or buy a good brand like Gim, Igor or Galbani, for example. SERVES 4

4 boneless steaks of your choice (rump, fillet, sirloin) *cultivated rocket leaves, washed*
olive oil *balsamic vinegar*
200 g creamy Gorgonzola, cut into 4 slices *salt and freshly ground black pepper*

PREHEAT THE GRILL TO VERY HOT. Brush the steaks with a little oil but don't salt them until the last second as the salt will cause the blood to leak out. Bear in mind that the Gorgonzola will be slightly salty, so you will not need much salt. Season also with the pepper at this point, then place the steaks under the grill and cook them according to your taste.

About 1 minute before the steaks are done, top each with a slice of Gorgonzola, thick enough so that, instead of melting and drizzling away to nothing, some of the cheese will melt and some will remain whole, but soft and warm and creamy on top.

Serve with a side salad of rocket, drizzled with olive oil and balsamic vinegar, which is sweeter than other vinegars and will accompany the cheese and steak very well.

Other leaves growing tips

LAMB'S LETTUCE Don't waste your money on pricey imported lamb's lettuce as it's easy to grow and quite quick from ground to plate. It can be sown from March to April and then again from July to the end of October, which is its main season. Many people are amazed that you can sow it so late in the year, but this is its time, so let nature take its course and you'll be eating this wonderful leaf in the autumn and winter, especially if you stagger the sowing. It won't grow back after you've picked it, so pull the whole bunch of leaves up, cut the small root off, wash, dress and serve. I always plant a lot of this wonderful leaf, as I love making salad just with lamb's lettuce. Sow 1 cm deep, water occasionally, especially at first, and nature will do the rest. It doesn't need full sun or feeding and pests pretty much leave it alone.

There are two main varieties:

Verte de Cambrai: The best-quality and most famous variety, which comes from north-west France. This region has made lamb's lettuce its own.

Valeriana d'Olanda: A Dutch variety with larger leaves than the Cambrai. I very much like this one; if the Cambrai is restaurant quality, then this is garden quality, which is fine. The larger, fatter leaf gives it a meatier bite, but the colour is a less attractive lighter green than the Cambrai. There is also a restaurant quality F1 version of this variety.

ROCKET is easy to grow as it's a single leaf that sticks out of the ground and grows quickly. It is prone to 'bolting', or going to seed. Luckily, though, the flowers are edible too, and they look very pretty in a salad. It has a long sowing season from March to August, so you can get lots of quick successive cuttings. You can grow it in a pot or in the ground, and a little seed goes a long way. The seed is tiny, like strawberry seed, so don't sow it on a windy day. It needs to be sprinkled just under the surface, ½ cm deep. Adding a little sand will help if you have heavy soil. It can suffer from a pest called flea beetle. This turns the leaves of your rocket into lace. They will be full of pin-sized holes with brown edges. Cut it back and resow, but don't dig it back into the soil as you'll attract even more flea beatle.

Cultivated Rocket: Also called salad rocket. It works like this: sow, eat, sow, eat, sow. It's an annual, and once you've picked it you'll need to resow. The leaves are larger than wild rocket leaves and the seed is much bigger too. It has a milder flavour and is the rocket we see and use most in the UK. Very easy to grow.

Wild Rocket: Technically a weed, so really easy to grow. It works like this: sow, eat, eat, eat, eat, etc. This is because if you leave some plants in the ground the seed will be scattered and will then come back spontaneously year after year. And it's not invasive like mint. A popular friend to have is wild rocket! It can be very peppery, and some people prefer it as a result. Wild rocket is the one you mostly get in Europe, and it can be expensive to buy in the shops. I often wish I was a wild-rocket grower because it's popular and people pay stunning prices for it.

Cucumbers and Gherkins Italian cukes are a different family from their British cousins, and in terms of flavour come somewhere between the melon and the cucumber. In Italy, we call them 'cetriolo melone', or cucumber melons, and the taste is more like cucumber when they are small and nearer melon as they get larger. So don't expect that classic cucumber sandwich flavour, but the Italian varieties are delicious in their own right. They can be used differently in the kitchen, they are very refreshing and also go better with meats.

Obviously, we've made cucumbers our own here in Britain, but they are eaten in almost every other country in the world, particularly in hot countries such as in the Middle East where their refreshing qualities (they are 95 per cent water) are greatly prized. They are used most successfully in Lebanese, Greek and Turkish food, where they are eaten with Feta cheese, olive oil, oregano and salt.

Cucumbers are diuretic and the minerals they contain (especially in the peel) have beneficial properties to skin and connective tissue, which is why they are often used in beauty products and why, traditionally, placing slices over tired eyes is recommended as a treatment.

Gherkins are very good to grow for children to eat fresh. My four-year-old calls them 'his cucumbers', because they are just his size! They are also easier and quicker to grow than regular cucumbers and instead of getting a few large fruits, you're going to get lots of little ones. It goes without saying that you can pickle them too and this way you will be able to preserve them in glass jars in the larder for up to a year.

To pickle gherkins is simple:
1. Follow the rules for sterilizing your jars (see page 206).
2. Wash and place the gherkins in a bowl and cover with sea salt to remove any excess water. Leave overnight.
3. Dry with a tea towel the following day and pack them into the jars as tightly as possible.
4. Fill with distilled malt vinegar, some whole peppercorns and some dill (as is the custom in eastern Europe, where the best pickled gherkins come from).

Insalata di Cetrioli e Feta

CUCUMBER AND FETA SALAD

This is actually a Slovakian side dish that I have adapted slightly, as I love the Greek way of eating Feta cheese with cucumbers. The saltiness of the cheese complements the juiciness and freshness of the cucumber. Don't be tempted to use balsamic vinegar for this recipe because we are adding sugar already and the dark colour will make the white cheese look grey and unattractive. Try this as a summer dish on its own or serve as a side dish with some doorstep sandwiches. SERVES 4

4 medium cucumbers, washed and peeled
4 tablespoons white wine vinegar
1 teaspoon salt
2 teaspoons sugar

200 g Feta cheese, cubed
paprika
4 tablespoons olive oil

IT IS IMPORTANT TO WASH THE CUCUMBERS even though you are peeling them. There may be earth on the skins and if you are handling them it is very important to make sure they are clean.

Cut the cucumbers into slices about 2 mm thick and put them into a bowl with the vinegar, salt and sugar. Check the seasoning and add more salt, sugar or vinegar to suit your tastes, bearing in mind that Feta cheese is salty.

When you are satisfied that the seasoning is balanced, divide the cucumber between four plates. Put the cubed Feta cheese on top, sprinkle on some paprika to taste – which will also give a lovely colour to the dish – and then, just before serving, add a tablespoon of olive oil per portion.

Cucumber and Gherkin growing tips

Cucumbers and gherkins should be started off in a pot and then planted in the greenhouse, or outside if the packet says that's OK. Italian cucumbers should be treated like a melon and grown in the greenhouse from start to finish. They'll climb around and look quite rustic, as do the fruits, so make sure you put some canes or wires for them to climb up and to keep the plants separate so they don't get overcrowded. Feed them with tomato food in the summer to give them a boost, especially if they're in growbags as these can become depleted very quickly. They do well against a trellis but you can grow them on the ground also. Set out transplants or sow direct a metre apart (3–5 seeds per station; thin to three best plants) with rows about 2 metres apart.

In Britain there are all-female varieties, but outside the UK this is not considered important and the varieties shown below all have male and female flowers. Here are some of the varieties I'm most familiar with.

Gherkin Piccolo di Parigi: The classic pickling gherkin in shape, size and texture, right down to the little goose bumps on the skin. This one is from Paris (we often refer to gherkins by their French name, 'cornichons'). Early variety. Harvest from July to end of October.

Gherkin White Wonder Bianco Primiticcio: White gherkins are often seen in Italy. Both the green and white varieties have similar characteristics and are very good eaten fresh. An early variety with few spines, which can be sown until August.

Gherkin Beth Alpha: These Middle Eastern type cucumbers have a very thin skin and a mild flavour with absolutely no bitterness. They are productive over a long season: one of the earliest to fruit and should keep going until a frost. In short, they are one of the best all-round gherkins/cucumbers available. Pick them when they are about 12–15 cm long for best flavour.

Marketmore: A British-style cucumber with few spines and of mid length. Mid/early, this is a very reliable variety to grow and a good eater.

Lungo Verde degli Ortolani: 'Long green cucumber of the veg grower'! An Italian variety of a British-style cucumber. Mid/late, dark green with smooth skin. Sow from March to July.

Tondo di Manduria: Looks much like a Crystal Apple variety. Mid/early with medium-sized round green fruits and juicy flesh. Rustic 'melon cucumber' variety. Sow from March to July and grow protected in the UK.

Carosello Medio Lungo Pugliese: A southern Italian variety, mid/early and with medium-sized fruits. Rustic 'melon cucumber' variety. Sow from March to July and grow protected in the UK.

Lungo Tortarello: A slightly strange 'melon cucumber' variety in that it will produce really nice-looking, long, slightly curved fruits, but the odd fruit will be completely covered in long fine hairs for no reason at all.

Radishes I like radishes quite a lot but don't think of them as being especially Italian. But then roast chicken isn't thought of as being Italian, and we eat that too! Radishes can be a bit limited in their uses because of their strong flavour. Of course they are a classic salad vegetable, but are also nice just eaten on their own with butter or salt.

Radishes come in different shapes and sizes, and strengths too. The general rule is that the white-tipped ones are more peppery and the red ones less, but then there are also yellow, black and white varieties (also known as mooli).

Radish growing tips

Radishes don't like the heat and can go to seed, so that's why they are sown in the spring and the autumn, but not during the summer. There are always exceptions to the rule though and this is the Polish Szlata (gold) radish variety, which can be sown continuously from spring to autumn. This is because it won't grow in the very cold Polish winters and so has adapted.

Flamboyant and French Breakfast: I have grouped these two varieties together as they are similar. They are both long radish varieties with white tips. Sow spring and autumn.

Szlata: I was at a show in Poland with Mr Franchi, and we were invited by the director of a Polish seed company on to their stand. On the table was a bottle of vodka. We were poured one and, not to offend, drank it down. Seven vodkas later, Mr Franchi stood up, a little worse for wear but stand he did, and the Polish director said with great satisfaction, 'You have represented your country well.' We left with this unusual yellow radish called Szlata added to our range (the Poles are particular experts on radishes and gherkins). Sow from spring to autumn continuously.

Rosso Burro Gigante: A Sardinian variety, the name translated literally means 'red buttery giant'. It is a radish of large dimensions, red, crunchy and of good flavour with medium strength. Sow spring and autumn.

Candelo di Fuoco and China Rose: The former translates as 'candle of fire'. Both of these are long red varieties, about 12 cm. They are quite peppery and thin, so although the mass is the same as a 'normal' radish, you will get small slices.

Rapid Red Sanova: An early round, red salad radish variety of medium size. Resistant to hollowing out. Sow in spring and autumn.

Candelo di Ghiaccio: 'White Icicle'. Long white radishes, sometimes called mooli.

Celery Celery contains minerals and vitamins, with very high levels of vitamin C, and has quite a high water content, which is why it is so juicy. It is said that celery can help lower blood pressure and may have important anti-cancer fighting agents. It is very good served with cream cheese or blue cheese and for dipping into bagna cauda. But it is also a constituent, with onion and carrot, of most Italian sauces, ragùs and sughi. Often, the sauce is liquidized so you don't see all the vegetables, but this is why these sauces are both tasty and wholesome.

Sedano con Formaggio Paglino
CELERY WITH PAGLINO CHEESE

Paglino is an amazing cheese from Piedmont – creamy, runny, mild, yet flavoursome – and it goes very well with celery, as do most creamy cheeses. In contrast to the superb-tasting Paglino, if you are using a bland cream cheese like Philadelphia, you can replace the olive oil with truffle oil and change the focus of the flavour. This is a simple and quick recipe. The grooves of celery were designed for cream cheese! SERVES 8 WITH APERITIFS

8 large celery sticks, washed   *12 black olives, chopped*
300 g Paglino cheese   *olive oil*

AFTER YOU'VE WASHED THE CELERY, make sure you dry it and remove any excess filaments running down the outside. Trim each end and spread the cheese into the grooves of the celery, starting at the wide end and leaving the thin end for holding. Make sure you don't overfill – the cheese should remain level with the edge of the celery.

Sprinkle the black olives on top and just gently firm them into the cheese. Drizzle with olive oil and arrange each one into half a paper napkin, so that they can be eaten without mess.

Celery growing tips

Rossa di Torino: An amazing variety with reddish stalks, found only in Turin. It must be blanched. The seed is hard to obtain as it is only produced locally, not commercially.

Dorato d'Asti: Another variety from the alpine region of Piedmont but this time with a golden stalk. It needs blanching and produces a large plant of juicy, fresh celery sticks.

Verde Pascal: A variety from Perpignan in France with green stalks. It doesn't need to be blanched and produces good-sized celery plants.

zucchine, zucche e zucchette

COURGETTES, PUMPKINS AND SQUASHES

Courgettes, pumpkins and squashes are all related members of the Cucuritacae family and they should be treated similarly.

While the British use the French 'courgette', the Italian 'zucchini' is the name used in America, Australia and New Zealand. As for pumpkins, we tend to associate them with countries like America, Australia, France and South Africa, where they are widely used and have good varieties, but both Britain and Italy grow and use pumpkin (zucca) only to a slightly lesser extent.

Courgettes Courgettes are extremely versatile and can be used small, medium or large, as marrows. In Italy we tend to pick the fruits smaller than is usual in Britain. They can be fried, roasted, mashed or boiled to use in soups and can also be stuffed or eaten raw.

NONNA ANGELA'S STUFFED ZUCCHINI

My nonna on my mother's side used to make these. Nonna Angela could speak two languages – London and Piedmontese – and she wasn't very good at either English or Italian. Every region in Italy has its own dialect, which changes from town to town and sometimes even from village to village, and my nonna came from Ivrea in Piedmont.

This is one of those dishes you can prepare in advance and then warm through. Or you can eat the courgettes cold the next day as part of a picnic as they are finger food too and this works well as an al fresco dish. I use long courgettes for this recipe, not round, even though the shape of the round ones makes them easier to stuff. The recipe calls for long ones, and I'm a real traditionalist – a trait shared by many Italians. It means we keep all our traditions and varieties and pass them down to the next generation, but we're therefore not keen to change recipes. I would die before I stuck Cheddar on pasta, for example, despite it being one of the best cooking cheeses in the world, but I'd rather have no cheese on my pasta than something other than what that particular recipe requires (and no cheese of any sort on pasta with seafood!).

You can drizzle olive oil flavoured with fresh lemons over the top of the filling to help the mixture stay moist, and olives or capers also work really well in the filling. SERVES 4

200 g ricotta cheese
1 onion, chopped
185 g canned tuna

salt and freshly ground black pepper
freshly grated Parmesan cheese, to taste
4 long medium courgettes (not marrows)

PREHEAT THE OVEN to Gas Mark 3/170°C.

Mix together the ricotta, onion and tuna, season and add grated Parmesan to taste.

Cut a small piece of skin from the straightest side of each courgette, so that they will sit better in the baking tray. Then cut a 'V' shape from the top of each courgette and heap the filling mixture into it. Place the piece that you cut out on top of the filling to help stop it drying out.

Put the stuffed courgettes in a baking tray and bake in the oven for about 30 minutes, until the courgettes are cooked through – if a skewer will push cleanly through a courgette, they are done.

CIRILLINI PASTA WITH TOMATO AND COURGETTE

by LetsgoItalian.com

Cirillini is the Italian name for small curly pasta tubes but you can use any pasta shape in this dish. Make this lovely, fresh-flavoured dish when you want something healthy and delicious after the excesses of Christmas. It's also a great way to get kids to eat courgettes! SERVES 4

200 g cirillini pasta

2 tablespoons extra-virgin olive oil

2 cloves of garlic, crushed

1 medium courgette, coarsely grated

pinch of dried chilli flakes

400 g can pomodorini cherry tomatoes

salt and freshly ground black pepper

fresh Parmesan cheese, to serve

BOIL THE PASTA in a large pan of lightly salted water for 7 minutes – drain thoroughly.

Meanwhile, heat the olive oil gently in a saucepan along with the crushed garlic. Add the grated courgette to the pan and sauté for 1–2 minutes. Add a pinch of dried chilli flakes followed by the pomodorini cherry tomatoes. Season and stir well. Cover the pan and simmer gently for 4–5 minutes. Add the cooked pasta to the pan and stir well to combine. Spoon into warmed serving bowls and grate over some fresh Parmesan. Serve immediately.

STUFFED COURGETTE FLOWERS by Giuseppe Silvestri, Head Chef, Harrods

ENOUGH FOR 6 PEOPLE AS A CRUNCHY STARTER

200 g ricotta

2 anchovies, chopped

grated Parmesan cheese

1 egg yolk

20 courgette flowers

vegetable oil for deep-frying

sea salt and freshly ground black pepper

For the batter

20 g yeast

100 g flour

75 ml water

50 ml beer

pinch of salt and freshly ground black pepper

MIX THE BATTER INGREDIENTS TOGETHER until smooth and leave for 30 minutes.

Mix together the ricotta, anchovies, grated Parmesan and egg yolk.

Clean the courgette flowers: take off the spiky bits at the base and the central pollen stem. Stuff the flowers with the ricotta mixture and gently twist each flower at the top to seal.

Dip the stuffed flowers in the batter and immediately deep-fry in hot vegetable oil. When light brown, remove and drain on kitchen paper to absorb excess oil. Sprinkle with sea salt and pepper and serve hot.

Zucchini a Scapece
SUN-DRIED COURGETTES WITH MINT AND GARLIC
by Ursula Ferrigno

This method of 'cooking', called a scapece, is very Neapolitan and is often applied to fish such as sardines as well as vegetables. Aubergines and strips of sweet pepper can be prepared in the same way. This dish can be eaten as a vegetable accompaniment or on its own. SERVES 6

9 large courgettes, topped and tailed
175 ml olive oil
a large handful of fresh mint leaves, coarsely
 chopped

3 cloves of garlic, finely chopped
6 tablespoons good-quality white wine vinegar
4 tablespoons extra-virgin olive oil
sea salt

CUT THE COURGETTES INTO SLICES LENGTHWAYS. Place them on a wooden board, cover with a cloth and leave in the sun to dry for about 3 hours. Alternatively, put them on a baking sheet in the oven at Gas Mark 1/110°C for about an hour to dry out completely without discolouring.

Heat the olive oil in a large pan and fry all the dry courgette slices, in batches if necessary, until golden. Don't bother to turn them over. Drain carefully on kitchen paper.

Transfer the courgette slices to a dish and sprinkle with the mint, garlic, vinegar, extra-virgin olive oil and salt. Cover and leave to stand in a cool place for at least 4 hours or overnight.

ZUCCHINI TRIFOLATI by Rose Gray, The River Cafe

Vegetables 'trifolati' is a method of slicing and cooking with garlic, olive oil and parsley. Other ingredients maybe added. Here we add fresh ripe tomatoes. SERVES 4

500 g courgettes
300 g cherry tomatoes
2 cloves of garlic
2 tablespoons basil leaves

2 tablespoons olive oil
extra-virgin olive oil
salt and freshly ground black pepper

WASH THE COURGETTES and cut in half lengthways and then into rough pieces of about 2 cm. Tear the tomatoes in half and squeeze out some of the seeds and juice. Peel and cut the garlic into slivers. Chop the basil.

Heat the olive oil in a frying pan. Add the courgettes and garlic, and stir to combine. When the courgettes begin to brown, add the tomatoes and salt and pepper. Stir well, and cook for a further 5 minutes. Remove from the heat and add the basil. Drizzle with extra-virgin olive oil and cover. Let sit for at least 10 minutes before serving.

Courgette growing tips

Courgettes, pumpkins and squashes all love fertile or manured ground. You often get courgettes growing in rich, dark compost heaps from half-eaten discarded fruits thrown in to rot down.

Sow courgettes, pumpkins and squashes 1 cm deep (2 cm for pumpkins) in pots with the seed upright, then plant outside after the last frosts. There are two reasons for doing this. First, frost will kill them, so they need protection until then. Secondly, the plants when small have soft, fine hairs like you get on the back of your neck. Slugs and snails will eat them when they are like this. But when the plants are bigger, these hairs will turn into rough bristles and the slugs won't touch the plants from then on.

Always water courgettes at their base, avoiding soaking the leaves, as this will lead to a white powdery mildew forming on them, which will shorten the life of the fruits but won't affect their flavour. Also, the plants will benefit from some tomato food in the summer, especially if they are growing in pots or containers, which can run out of food fairly quickly.

Marrows are essentially big courgettes, although I'll probably get some disagreement with that comment. Some varieties make better marrows than others, with Striato probably being the best. Marrows are generally not grown on purpose in Italy and are often seen only as the 'one that got away', hidden under a leaf! That said, 'waste not, want not' kicks in, and the marrow will be baked and served with a drizzle of olive oil and Parmesan, or stuffed and then baked.

Courgettes really are a truly regional species in Italy with almost every region having its own variety. There are examples from Venice-Friuli, Bologna, Florence, Rome, Naples, Milan, Sicily, Piacenza, Genova, Tuscany and Sarzana, with each region cooking its own courgettes differently. There are also two national varieties (Striato and Verde), and the round courgette from Nice across the border is also widely used. In contrast, British varieties are now, regrettably, truly standardized and you'll most likely end up with Defender or Eight Ball as stock choices. Different courgettes have different characteristics and uses. For example, the round courgettes from Piacenza and Nice are usually stuffed, the courgette from Bologna is shaped like a rugby ball and makes large slices, so it's great for frying.

Striato d'Italia: This is what you think of when someone says 'zucchini' – a real classic. Each plant produces about 5 kg of fruits and the main criticism I hear about Striato is that people get fed up with eating them all the time, they are so productive. The excellent-quality stripey fruits are best picked small to medium sized.

Verde d'Italia: Another national example, producing fruits that are best picked small to medium sized. A very reliable producer of good-quality fruits.

Bolognese: From Bologna, this variety is bloated like a small rugby ball.

Romanesco: 'Of Rome', this is the variety you most often see picked finger-sized with the flower still attached. They have slight ridges, a nutty flavour and are also good producers of flowers.

Nero di Milano: This is a black-skinned variety (actually the skin is such a dark green that it just looks black), hence its name 'Black of Milan'. We are used to seeing these 'black' types in Britain, but in Italy they are not used so much outside Milan. They are perceived as being not as tasty and sometimes having bitter skins. Actually, Nero is a good all-rounder but isn't as creamy in consistency as lighter-skinned varieties. Pick medium sized for best results.

Genovese: One of my favourite varieties along with the Romanesco. It's got a really creamy consistency and is great for making Zucchini Trifolati.

Striato di Napoli: An older variety than the Striato d'Italia but quite similar in habit and characteristics.

Tondo di Piacenza: A round courgette from Piacenza (near Parma), which is super stuffed with local Parma ham and Parmesan cheese and then baked. Round courgettes are good for baking whole, slicing and stuffing, so very versatile.

Tondo di Nizza: Aka 'Rond de Nice', this light green, round courgette is from just across the border from Ventimiglia. Like the Tondo from Piacenza, a good all-rounder and very versatile in the kitchen. A very well-known and popular variety in Britain, where it has been available for many years.

Lungo Bianco: This is a Sicilian trailing variety with skin so light green it is known as 'long white'. The fruits are slightly curved and will tolerate dryer conditions.

Albarello di Sarzana: A light green fattish variety that stuffs well, although long courgettes need propping up when cooking. Medium creamy consistency and quite juicy.

Rugoso Friulana: A real ugly duckling from the Venice-Friuli area that borders Yugoslavia. Yellow, rough, misshapen and warty, this variety stays firmer when cooked, making it ideal for dishes that need longer cooking times, like Peperonata for example.

Lungo Fiorentino: The first time I ever spoke to The River Cafe, they asked whether I sold this variety. It produces quality, light green, slightly ribbed fruits with superb flavour. It also produces lots of flowers. Although the name means 'long of Florence', don't pick it too large.

Blackjack F1: A hybrid F1 black-skinned variety. Although hybrids are more expensive to produce, so you get less seed in the packs, they tend to be reliable and very productive, and Blackjack is no exception.

Zucchino da Fiore: This variety is called San Pasquale and it comes from Tuscany. It is unusual in that it produces a good quantity of flowers and not so many fruits, so it is used almost exclusively for the flowers, which are stuffed, battered and fried or used in omelettes and frittata.

Pumpkins Pumpkin is a very versatile vegetable: you can roast it, mash it and make pumpkin pie, chutney and jam. In Mantua they make a sweet pumpkin ravioli with raisins, amaretti biscuits and cinnamon. These are boiled for a short time and served with butter – delicious.

To roast pumpkin whole, simply put it in the oven at Gas Mark 4/180°C until tender. Test it by pushing a skewer through. If it goes through easily, it's cooked. Pumpkins vary greatly in size, but you will need at least an hour to cook an 'average' sized example. You can also cut pumpkin into slices, drizzle with olive oil, seasoning and fresh thyme, and bake in the oven for about 30 minutes, depending on size. Add potatoes, butternut squash and carrots, bearing in mind that potatoes take longer to cook so first cut them into 5–7.5 cm pieces.

Pumpkins have a high sugar content, making them ideal for dishes like soup. I find butternut squashes too sweet for soup, but they are excellent for other dishes where their sweetness shines through.

MARINA DI CHIOGGIA CAPONATA by Neil Haydock, Fifteen, Cornwall

This is a great winter alternative to the regular caponata made with aubergine throughout the summer. It goes very well with grilled chicken, pheasant and venison. SERVES 2–4

light olive oil for frying
1 pumpkin (Marina di Chioggia), peeled and diced into 1.5 cm cubes
150 g onion, chopped
2 cloves of garlic, chopped
100 ml red wine vinegar

200 g can chopped tomatoes
100 g sultanas (plump and juicy)
a small handful of flat-leaf parsley
a small handful of celery leaves
sea salt and freshly ground black pepper

HEAT A FRYING PAN and add a small amount of oil and then the pumpkin. Season lightly and allow to colour a little while stirring occasionally. When almost cooked, remove from the pan, drain and reserve.

Add a little oil to a heated saucepan, then the onion and garlic, and sweat gently until soft. Increase the temperature and add the vinegar. Allow this to reduce until almost dry, then add the tomatoes and sultanas and cook for 5 minutes. Add the pumpkin and cook until tender. Season the mix and add the chopped parsley and celery leaves.

Allow to cool and serve at room temperature or chill and refrigerate overnight and allow to come up to room temperature before serving.

My dad, Vincenzo, was so proud of his little Italian deli in Hendon.
He served the food as it should be served – not necessarily how the customers wanted it!

Frittata dell'Orto

ROASTED VEGETABLE FRITTATA

A frittata is a rustic omelette and this one is definitely speciality 'de la maison' because you can vary the ingredients, but the basic method stands. Left-over roasted veg – potatoes, pumpkin, onion, beetroot, butternut squash – are very good to use, so if you're going to roast some vegetables, make extra with the idea of making frittata the following day. It's also a great way to use up the culo, or ends, of ham, salami and cheese.

The trick to cooking a good frittata is just a question of timing. Do the things that take the longest first. The aim is to have everything just cooked properly as the eggs set. As this is a homely dish, don't spend time finely slicing the onion or making sure the pieces of ham are all the same size and shape. Indeed, the unevenness will contribute to the final texture and flavour, with some pieces being crisp and others not. SERVES 4

vegetable oil
2 large potatoes and the same weight of pumpkin,
*   or left-over roasted vegetables, cut into bite-*
*   sized pieces*
1 onion, roughly chopped
100 g ham, salami, mortadella or speck, cut up
8 eggs
a dash of milk or cream

fresh tarragon
a knob of butter
2 cloves of garlic, roughly chopped
a cupful of peas
cheese (Provolone, Cheddar, Toma, Fontina) in the
*   quantity you like, cut into cubes*
salt and freshly ground black pepper

PUT A GOOD SPLASH OF VEGETABLE OIL IN A PAN and, if you are using left-over roasted veg, throw them in to sizzle, along with the onion and ham or salami. If you are not using left-overs, cook the potatoes a little first then add the pumpkin, as it will take less time to cook. You'll need to season the potatoes and pumpkin – left-over vegetables may not need any.

Fry on a medium heat to get some golden edges on the vegetables and salami and caramelize the onions a touch, which will give the dish a lovely colour and super flavour, but keep tossing the ingredients around to prevent them burning.

While the vegetables are cooking (about 4–6 minutes), break the eggs into a jug and add a good dash of milk or cream, tarragon (to taste) and the butter in little pieces.

Add the garlic and the peas to the pan and cook for a minute before adding the egg mixture, which you should season just before pouring into the pan, otherwise it will go runny. Spread the pieces of cheese evenly so that everyone will get some. Don't grate the cheese – it's a frittata not an omelette, and each mouthful should be different: one cheesy, the next beautiful roasted potato, the next caramelized onion, etc.

Keep the heat at medium and cover with a good lid that will trap the heat and set the top while keeping it moist and melting the cheese. Don't turn the heat down low and cook it for ages or it will go rubbery, and don't try to cook it quickly over a very high heat as the bottom will burn and the top will still be runny.

That's it – when it's just set on top, bring the pan to the table (protected with a heat-resistant mat or covering). If you like, you can brown the top by putting it under a hot grill for a minute before serving but make sure your pan is grill-proof and the handle won't melt.

To serve, make sure there are a couple of essentials on the table: rustic bread cut into wedges and butter pieces. Don't use packaged bread – what a waste of a good frittata. It would be like wearing a Zegna or Armani suit with really cheap trainers. Don't serve tea with it unless you live in a transport café. A light white wine is perfect.

Riso con la Zucca
PUMPKIN RICE, Lina Stores, Soho, London

SERVES 4

500 g arborio rice
200 g pumpkin, peeled and diced
salt

50 g butter
2 tablespoons grated Parmesan cheese

BOIL THE RICE and the pumpkin together in salted water until tender. Drain and mash the pumpkin into the rice. Add the butter and Parmesan and mix well. Serve piping hot.

'Il vino e' buono dove l'ostessa e' bella'

THE WINE IS ALWAYS GOOD WHERE THE HOSTESS IS BEAUTIFUL

Pumpkin growing tips

Different pumpkins have different characteristics and some are better for some purposes than others, so check under each variety listed below that you are growing the right one. No point growing a dry pumpkin if you want to make jam, or a jam pumpkin if you want it for roasting.

They should be treated like courgettes, sown first (2 cm deep) into pots or trays, and then transplanted out when the risk of frosts has passed. They love manure or rich dark soil from the compost heap. They should be watered from the base to avoid white powdery mildew forming on the leaves and fed in the summer with some tomato food, especially if they are sown into growbags. Personally, I would plant two per growbag instead of three as they are hungry beasts. Well, they have pretty large fruits to produce, after all!

Pumpkins are pretty easy to grow, but remember they are 'trailing' and will run. You can use this to your advantage by growing them upwards instead of along the ground, say up on to a shed. The plants do have little 'grapplers' that will hold on to whatever it is they are climbing up, but you could support them by using some twine or wire. Don't be tempted to tie this too tight around the growing stem as you need to allow some room to expand. Imagine if you didn't change your sweater between the ages of five and eighteen... Plants are no different!

Marina di Chioggia: A super pumpkin from the Veneto (Venice) region of Italy. Produces medium-sized fruits with grey/green knobbly skin and sweet orange flesh. A good all-rounder and a permanent resident of my veg plot.

Delica F1: A small green-skinned variety of superb quality. So good is it that it is sold in Italy by name. A pure culinary pumpkin, and because it's small you are not overloaded with pumpkin for every meal for a week!

Padana: A yellow and green pumpkin with yellow flesh and of good dimensions. It is on the drier side but not too much, and this does make it good for pumpkin pie, ravioli and mash. From the alpine north-west of Italy.

Berrettina Piacentina: A mid/early pumpkin producing medium to large fruits that are squashed at their poles. The skin is greeny grey, knobbly and firm, and the flesh is yellowy orange and sweet. This is one of the best pumpkins for making Mantuan pumpkin ravioli.

Jam Pumpkin da Marmellata: Mid/early with French origins and very sweet flesh, this variety is used to make preserves. Because the pumpkin is sweet, less sugar is needed, and added lemon zest gives the jam a fresh flavour. The fruits are orange with a smooth skin and are flattened at the poles.

Quintale: The name literally means 'tonne' in English, and the reward for growing it is large, orange fruits of reasonable quality and flavour for its size. Large pumpkins can be very decorative and they also go a long way. Imagine how much delicious pumpkin soup one of these beautiful fruits will give you.

Rouge d'Etampes: Mid/late French pumpkin with flat 'squat' fruits that are slightly scalloped. Sweet orange and meaty flesh. A popular garden variety.

Halloween: A classic small to mid-sized variety for making doorstep lanterns for Halloween. It is of average quality, OK to eat but nothing special, but it is reliable and stores well.

Muscade de Provence: A vigorous, medium-sized example from the south of France. The skin is green, turning yellow after harvesting, and heavily scalloped. It has very sweet and meaty orange flesh, a good flavour and is a very good storer.

Lunga di Napoli: The fruits of this Neapolitan monster can reach a metre in length and look like long, green butternut squashes. You get particularly good, even-sized slices from this variety and it is easier to peel, being long and smooth rather than rounded and knobbly.

Hubbard Large Blue: A relation of the Hubbard True Green and a good storing variety. It produces lush foliage and is a good producer of mid-sized, wrinkled, greeny blue, pear-shaped fruits.

Hubbard True Green: A late American pumpkin that forms unusual medium-sized, pear-shaped, knobbly fruits. The skin is pastel green, turning yellow after harvesting. It has very sweet and meaty orange flesh and is a very good storer.

Atlantic Giant: American gargantuan of the pumpkin world, producing record-breaking orange scalloped fruits, which can reach in excess of a quarter of a tonne. Great talking point, but not a great eater.

Mammoth: Mid/late. Luxuriant plant of good productivity, which produces yellow-skinned fruits, round but flattened at its poles and with meaty, sweet yellow flesh.

peperoni e peperoncini

PEPPERS AND CHILLIES

Peppers are to be found in every shape, size and colour imaginable, not to mention sweetness and heat.

Of course the term 'hot' is relative and what is hot to a Calabrian and to a Jamaican may be totally different, and a matter for much debate! There is an old saying: 'The poorer the soil, the hotter the chilli', and this one, apparently, is proven. The whole purpose of a plant's life is reproduction. If conditions are harsh, the chilli plant will make as many fruits as possible, and the fruits will be hot to deter the birds.

Sweet Peppers Oddly enough, the best peppers in Italy come from the Alps – Piedmont to be precise, Asti, Cuneo and Carmagnola to be really on the nail. The peppers that are widely available in the UK are an embarrassment: the fist-sized, standardized, mass-produced, hydroponically grown bought ones aren't a patch on the football-sized, misshapen, naturally grown ones you get in every supermarket and shop on the Continent. The only plus with the ones we buy in Britain is that they are small enough to stuff.

ROASTED PEPERONATA by Antony Worrall Thompson

A great salad from Apulia in southern Italy, which can be served as part of an antipasti selection. I'm not keen on pepper skins so I've adapted this classic dish. SERVES 4–6

3 onions, sliced

2 tablespoons extra-virgin olive oil

4 cloves of garlic, finely chopped

3 red peppers, roasted, peeled and sliced

3 yellow peppers, roasted, peeled and sliced

3 plum tomatoes, peeled, deseeded and diced

4 anchovy fillets, diced

1 hot chilli, finely diced

25 g baby capers, rinsed

6 basil leaves, ripped

3 tablespoons chopped flat-leaf parsley

1 tablespoon balsamic vinegar

salt and freshly ground black pepper

IN A LARGE FRYING PAN cook the onions in olive oil with the garlic until the onions have softened without colour, about 8–10 minutes.

Add the peppers, tomatoes, anchovies, chilli and capers and cook for a further 10 minutes.

Fold in the basil, parsley and balsamic vinegar. Season to taste.

Serve hot or at room temperature.

L'bun cusine' a tasta set volte'

THE GOOD COOK TASTES SEVEN TIMES

PEPERONATA

Made with yellow and red peppers and cooked slowly. There are many variations to this recipe but this is my version and, while some people will say that you shouldn't put courgette in peperonata, that is how I was taught to make it. The courgette bulks it out and tones down the strong flavour of the peppers a little. Quantities and cooking times may vary depending on the size of the peppers, so be flexible. For a really rich peperonata, at the end of cooking remove from the heat for a few minutes and stir in an egg. We do this at home when eating this dish on its own, with warm home-made bread. SERVES 4

olive oil

1 red onion (Rossa of Genova), thinly sliced

2 large yellow peppers (Giallo d'Asti), cut into rough chunks

2–3 red peppers (Corno Rosso), cut into rough chunks

1 courgette (Striato d'Italia), cut into thick slices

1 clove of garlic, crushed (optional)

1 tablespoon chicken stock

4 tomatoes (Roma), peeled, deseeded and chopped

salt and freshly ground black pepper

HEAT SOME OLIVE OIL IN A PAN and soften the onion. Add the peppers, courgette, garlic (if using) and stock and simmer gently, uncovered, for 20 minutes. Add the tomatoes and simmer for an additional 20 minutes, or until thick and shiny. Season to taste.

Peperone Imbottiti
STUFFED PEPPERS

You can also add minced pork to this filling, bound with an egg. SERVES 4

4 large sweet peppers

1 onion, chopped

olive oil

a handful of parsley, chopped

150 g breadcrumbs

50 g Pecorino cheese, grated

2 anchovies, chopped

20 g capers

salt and freshly ground black pepper

CLEAN THE PEPPERS by cutting around the stalk at the top, removing it and scraping out the seeds inside the pepper with a spoon. Wash carefully and dry upside down.

In a saucepan, soften the chopped onion in olive oil, remove to a bowl and add a handful of parsley, the breadcrumbs, cheese, chopped anchovies and capers and season to taste. Stuff the peppers with this mixture and drizzle a little good olive oil into each pepper. Place them in an oiled ovenproof dish, and bake for about 40 minutes at Gas Mark 4/180°C. Serve hot or cold.

Pepper growing tips

Always start peppers off between February and May, protected (on a windowsill, in a heated greenhouse, conservatory etc.), sowing them 1 cm deep in pots or yogurt tubs. They must have full light and heat at this point. When there is no more risk of frosts, you can plant them out into the greenhouse.

Some peppers can be grown outside – in a hot summer, all peppers will be OK outside (that's gardening for you, no constants). In the UK, bell peppers usually need a greenhouse: big peppers, big energy, big sun, big food, big water – these are hungry beasts. A Corno di Toro on the other hand is a bit more forgiving, and if you start them off early enough, they will grow outside in a sheltered sunny spot and produce good-quality, meaty red and yellow peppers.

All peppers start off green. Some stay green, but most will mature to either red or yellow and some novelty varieties range from purple and bright orange to cream. Gastronomically, I'm always wary of these gimmicky types, unless they are heirloom or traditional varieties – it's the purist in me, I guess, and looks and flavour don't always go together.

Corno Rosso and Dulce Italiano: Classic pepper, often referred to as 'Corno di Toro' ('Bull's Horn'). These peppers are still meaty and a good size, but a lot more forgiving than a bell pepper, and you are much more likely to have success growing these. Good all-round peppers, but bell peppers stuff better because of their shape.

Corno Giallo: Exactly the same as the red Bull's Horn, but it's yellow. Yellow peppers always cost more than red or green ones as they are considered sweeter.

Frigitello: Often called Friariello peppers, these are famous sweet peppers from Naples. They are pan-fried in olive oil, salted with sea salt and eaten with beer. You tell me what could be better than that!

Goccia d'Oro: A mid/early, rustic Bull's Horn variety, producing fruits of medium dimensions. The pepper has three to four lobes with a pale green to yellow colour, maturing red. It has fairly thick walls and very sweet flesh.

Giallo d'Asti: From the Piedmontese Alps, this variety is considered to be one of the finest peppers in Italy. It is yellow with three large lobes; it's very meaty and has a super flavour. This is one of the main varieties you should use for making Peperonata.

Carmagnola: Again from Piedmont, this is a large red pepper with four lobes and is the type of pepper you'll see on the markets the size of rugby balls.

Rosso d'Asti: A large red pepper from Asti, not so far from Carmagnola, and again a superb four-lobed variety for the greenhouse. A very good variety for using with the dish Bagna Cauda.

Topepo: An RHS Award of Garden Merit winner, this red variety looks like a scalloped beef tomato and, because it is flat-based, it stuffs really well. Medium-sized and very meaty.

Chilli Peppers The first chillies to reach Europe arrived around 1493 as a result of Colombus's voyages to the Americas. People don't always associate chillies with Italy, but they have a deep-rooted place in our culture, especially in the south. From the time that the Romans were trading throughout their empire, Italy has always been a melting pot of different races and cultures from all over Europe and the Middle East, and even the Far East. So it is no surprise that chillies are much favoured in Sicily and the south of Italy in particular, where there was a strong Arab influence. For example, dishes like Spaghetti alla Puttanesca come from Campagna, Peperoncini Ripieni from Calabria and Cima di Rape al Peperoncino from Puglia.

Peperoncini Ripieni
STUFFED CHILLI PEPPERS by Marco Centonze

This is a particularly popular antipasto in southern Italy, where it is treated as a real delicacy. The chillies used to look like large cherry tomatoes and, although hot to start with, lose much of their fieriness in the cooking process while retaining a deliciously sweet, fruity flavour. Although you can find the hot peppers in speciality greengrocers nowadays, we highly recommend buying the seeds and growing them yourself. Go for Franchi seeds and buy either the Red Cherry Small or Ciliegia Piccante for best results. SERVES 2 PER PERSON AS A STARTER

500 g fresh cherry chillies
1 litre water
1 litre white wine vinegar
3–4 anchovies in oil, chopped

200 g canned tuna in oil
1 heaped tablespoon small capers in vinegar
25 g freshly chopped parsley
500 ml extra-virgin olive oil

WASH THE CHILLIES WELL and, using a sharp paring knife, remove the tops, leaving a hole big enough to insert a small spoon and remove all the seeds.

Bring the water and vinegar to the boil in a pan. Place the cleaned, deseeded chillies in the boiling mixture for 5 minutes, then drain and leave to cool for a few minutes. Add the chopped anchovies to the drained tuna, capers and chopped parsley in a mixing bowl. Using a fork, crush and mix the ingredients until you're left with a medium-textured paste. You can use a food processor to do this but don't over-blend the mixture.

Take the drained chillies and, using your fingers, stuff them with the tuna paste, taking care not to overfill them. Pack the stuffed chillies closely in a sterilized 500 ml Kilner jar and cover with the extra-virgin olive oil.

Seal the jar and place in the fridge for 24 hours before enjoying with a good piece of crusty bread and a crisp glass of your favourite white wine (we recommend Greco Di Tufo from Naples!). The chillies should keep for at least a month in the fridge.

A photo from the 1950s showing how the seed packets were filled by hand with a teaspoon of seeds, then glued shut and left to dry.

Chilli pepper growing tips

There are many, many varieties of chilli in the world, so again I am featuring the ones I am familiar with through my work as a seedsman.

Adorno: An early, very hot Italian variety. A compact plant with greeny violet leaves. Dark green fruits that grow upwards and ripen to reddish violet. Can also be grown in containers.

Ciliegia Piccante: A mid/early, hot variety from Calabria. This compact plant has good foliage and produces small round fruits that turn deep red when ripe. They have a solid, tasty flesh and are ideal for stuffing and preserving. Traditionally they are filled with tuna and capers or anchovies and preserved in jars of olive oil. You can find these in any good Italian deli.

Jalapeno: A mid/early, hot variety from Mexico. It produces medium-long green fruits that are quite meaty, juicy and tasty. Used widely in the whole of the Americas and one of the best-known Mexican varieties in the world.

Cayenna: A mid/early, hot variety (ours are from Italy but they can be produced in other countries too). The plant is made up of lots of branches with small leaves. It produces a great many classic long, thin, deep green fruits, which turn red when ripe. Can be used fresh, dried or dried and ground to make cayenne pepper.

Stromboli: An early, hot variety from Italy, named after the famous volcano in the province of Sicily. A compact plant that produces bunches of conical dark green fruits that grow upwards, turning orange when ripe.

Etna: An early, hot variety from Italy. A compact plant that produces bunches of conical dark green fruits that.grow upwards, turning bright red when ripe.

Red Cherry Calabrese: An early, hot variety from Calabria, also called Piccante Calabrese. A very good stuffing chilli, superb filled with mozzarella and anchovies and placed under the grill.

Grisù F1: An early, hot variety from Sardinia. Vigorous medium-sized plant that produces meaty, dark green, cone-shaped fruits, turning red when ripe.

Pimiento de Padron: One of the best varieties. Mid/early, mild and from Galicia in Spain. The medium-sized bushy plant produces medium conical fruits that turn red when ripe (but are also eaten green). Meaty and very tasty, they are traditionally pan-fried in olive oil, sprinkled with a little sea salt, and eaten with beer. You eat the whole thing and are left with just the stalk in your hand. Depending on the time of year, one chilli in five or ten could be hot.

Romanian Giallo: An early, hot variety from Romania. A vigorous, compact plant that produces small, long, conical light green fruits that turn yellow when ripe. Very attractive.

brassica

BRASSICAS

Some brassicas have a bad reputation for being both boring and smelly, and while there is some truth in this, it doesn't make for the most inspiring of intros! But I'm pleased to report that they also have quite a few things going in their favour.

Firstly, there are some fantastic recipes for turning even the most humble of this family into excellent dishes. There is also the fact that this is one of those groups of vegetables that, generally speaking, you sow in the summer to grow on into the cold.

Then there are the health benefits of eating these greens in the winter months. In the past, before the days of fridges and supermarkets, this was even more important, and many illnesses, and hunger too, would have been avoided because of the availability of brassicas in the sparse winter months.

Cabbage This is one of those strange vegetables that children hate but, as they grow up, they turn out to like! It is often treated rather boringly, yet as an ingredient in other dishes, such as Sauerkraut or Coleslaw, it is surprisingly good. I also like cabbage braised and dressed with some soy sauce. Cabbages serve up well with the addition of sweet ingredients. For example, braised red cabbage with apple and bacon is really surprisingly good and makes a super accompaniment to venison.

Cavolo Verza Ripieni
STUFFED SAVOY CABBAGE LEAVES

As a child the only way I liked Savoy cabbage was in Italy, when I ate the leaves stuffed. Now Savoy cabbages remind me of my youth and, although I enjoy them boiled, served hot with a little soy sauce, I still really love eating them stuffed. The leaves are very large but quite pliable, which means that they won't break when you roll them up, but I find it helps to blanch them for a minute in boiling water or even to pour a kettle full of boiling water over the separated leaves. You can make these in advance and reheat them, even in a microwave, for a tasty but quick dinner. SERVES 4

a small sprig of rosemary	10–12 black olives, roughly chopped
olive oil	4 tablespoons beef stock
500 g minced pork	4 tablespoons grated Parmesan cheese
1 large onion, chopped	8 Savoy cabbage leaves
2 cloves of garlic, crushed	salt and freshly ground black pepper

HEAT THE ROSEMARY IN SOME OLIVE OIL in a frying pan, then fry the meat for a couple of minutes. Add the onion, garlic and olives, season and fry for another couple of minutes. It's important that the filling is properly seasoned as the cabbage is fairly bland. Add the stock, which will add more flavour and keep the meat moist, and cook until the meat is completely cooked through. Add some grated Parmesan at this point, stir it in and leave the mixture to cool.

Blanch the cabbage leaves in boiling water for 1 minute and remove with a slotted spoon. Lay each leaf out flat, divide the filling into eight equal portions and place a portion in the middle of each leaf. Roll up the leaves like a cigar, folding the ends in before you roll the last bit and secure with a wooden toothpick to ensure they don't open. If you prefer, you can make parcels instead of rolls by folding in the four corners and securing with a toothpick.

Reheat in the microwave for a few minutes at maximum power until they are hot through. Alternatively, you can heat them on a gentle heat in a covered frying pan with a little oil to stop them sticking and a couple of tablespoons of water to keep them from drying out. Again, make sure they are hot through before serving.

Rotolo di Platessa alla Verra e Prosecco

PLAICE FILLETS ROLLED IN CABBAGE with Prosecco Sauce

by Aldo Zilli

This recipe, if you have the time, is quite fantastic. Any sparkling wine will do if you can't find Prosecco, or even white wine, so give it a go and really impress your friends. SERVES 4

25 g butter
1 small onion, finely chopped
1 clove of garlic, finely chopped
3 sun-dried tomatoes, chopped
3 tablespoons chopped lemon thyme
50 g wholemeal breadcrumbs
juice of 1 lemon
8 large cabbage leaves
8 small plaice fillets
salt and freshly ground black pepper

For the Prosecco sauce
1 bottle of Prosecco
a pinch of saffron (optional)
3 tablespoons olive oil
3 banana shallots, roughly chopped
1 clove of garlic, crushed
1/2 lemon grass stalk, smashed
200 ml fish stock
250 ml double cream
juice of 1 lemon

FIRST MAKE THE STUFFING. Place the butter in a pan and let it melt over the heat and begin to froth. Add the onion and garlic and sauté, stirring, for 3–4 minutes until soft. Remove from the heat. Then add the tomatoes, thyme, breadcrumbs and lemon juice. Season to taste and set aside to cool.

Put the cabbage leaves into boiling, salted water for 2 minutes until al dente, then plunge into iced water and pat dry. Place a cabbage leaf on to a piece of cling film and lightly season with salt and pepper (make sure the cling film is slightly larger than the cabbage). Put a plaice fillet on top of the cabbage (again making sure the cabbage leaf is larger than the fish). Put a small ball of the cooled stuffing mix on to one end of the plaice and, holding the cling film, roll up tightly; be sure that the cling film remains on the outside only. Repeat with the remaining cabbage leaves and fish, to give two rolls per portion.

Pour the bottle of Prosecco into a pan and reduce by three-quarters to intensify the flavour. Add the saffron at this stage if you have it.

Steam the fish in the cling film parcels for approximately 12–15 minutes. Heat the olive oil in a separate pan and slowly pan-fry the shallots, garlic and lemon grass for 4–5 minutes until soft. Add the reduced Prosecco and fish stock to this mix and reduce again by one third. Add the double cream and reduce by one third again. Squeeze in some lemon juice and season with salt and pepper to taste. Pass through a sieve. Remove the cling film from the fish and slice each roll in half so you can see the layers. Pour the sauce over the fish and serve.

Brassica growing tips

Most brassicas actually need a frost to make them mature and taste better. It's no accident that Brussels sprouts are eaten for Christmas and not Easter. Thus, most varieties and cultivars in this family group are sown from May to the end of July, but, as my French teacher used to say when talking about verbs, 'There is always the exception'. Maceratese cauliflowers can be sown in January and Cima di Rapa broccoletti from April until the end of August. They don't require full sun, but they are going to grow through the winter slowly and every little bit will help.

Cabbages should be sown from May to July 1 cm deep, or the slugs will definitely have them before you do. Plant them out into the garden and I recommend that you cover them with some mesh to stop caterpillars breeding on them and decimating your crop.

Cuor di Bue Grosso: Often referred to commonly as 'Sweetheart' cabbages due to their shape, the name translates to 'ox's heart', which is also a good description. It is a medium-sized green cabbage with tightly wrapped leaves.

Langedijk and Copenhagen: These are traditional, late, round cabbages of good dimensions with compact heads. Harvest till around the end of December.

Red Cabbage Testa Nera: Red cabbages resist cold even more than green ones do. This variety is mid/late with a tightly wrapped head.

Golden Star F1: An early, green variety with a short stalk and a consistent, round medium-sized head. Harvest till around the end of December.

Penca Povoa Verde: Early. A very unusual variety that has huge leaves with large white ribs, looking not too dissimilar to Swiss chard. The head will close to form a round head like other cabbages. Sow from February right through to September. Harvest until the end of December.

Savoy Cabbage: These have heavily veined leaves that can be green or grey with a red flush. They will need some cold to mature. Varieties differ, but generally speaking they can be harvested between December and February.

Pasqualino: An early variety with a round, well-closed head of good dimensions. The leaves are large, blistered and intense green with subtle white veining. Harvest until the end of January.

San Michele: Mid/late. The cold and very beautiful city of Verona is the home of this variety, which is similar in appearance to Autumn King. It has a firm, violet-coloured head and is resistant to low temperatures. Harvest until the end of January.

Mantovano: This late variety comes from Mantua. It has a very large green head with white veining and can be harvested until the end of January.

Princess F1: Mid/early, this variety has a short stalk and a good-sized, round green head that is resistant to splitting or cracking.

Cauliflower One of those winter vegetables you find in every country of the world in different shapes, sizes and colours. In Britain, we mostly use white or cream-coloured cauliflowers, and who could possibly resist a cauliflower cheese in winter time, made with a rich, creamy sauce full of strong Cheddar? Even the most reluctant veg-eating child couldn't refuse.

THIMI TARKARI MASALA by Cyrus Rustom Todiwala

This originates from Nepal but has been absorbed by several hotels and restaurants, each claiming to have the original and be the best.

We have tried to bring about something simple, tasteful and easy to replicate and prepare. There are a few variations that make the dish more nutritious than is normally prepared by our industry. For instance it is common practice to simply deep-fry the vegetables in a lot of oil, which then makes the dish greasy and non-appetizing. It is essential that all of us put on our creative hats when cooking and make minor adjustments to suit our likes and dislikes. SERVES 4

8–10 cauliflower florets

1 large stem broccoli

1 heaped teaspoon sugar

1 medium carrot, diced

250–300 ml vegetable oil

1 medium onion, chopped

2 tablespoons ginger and garlic paste

2 teaspoons geera powder

½ teaspoon chilli powder

½ teaspoon crushed lovage (ajowan)

½ teaspoon turmeric (haldi)

½ teaspoon garam masala

¼ teaspoon crushed black peppercorns

1 teaspoon freshly squeezed lime or lemon juice

150–200 ml single cream

1 heaped tablespoon chopped coriander

salt

CUT THE CAULIFLOWER AND BROCCOLI into small florets. Cut the stems into tiny dice so that they can cook quickly along with the florets.

Bring just enough water to cover the broccoli and cauliflower to the boil in a saucepan and add a little salt and the sugar. Add the carrot and, when it is less than half done, add the broccoli and cauliflower. Boil for 2–3 minutes until all three are just half cooked. Drain in a colander over another bowl and reserve the liquid. Run some cold water over the vegetables to prevent them from carrying on cooking.

Heat the oil in a casserole or kadhai and, when hot, fry the three vegetables a little at time for just a minute or so and drain over another bowl. Make sure the oil is really hot, otherwise the vegetables will absorb too much. Pass the oil through a strainer and reserve for future use.

Wipe the casserole with kitchen paper, add 2 tablespoons of the reserved oil and heat. Add the onion and sauté until light brown. Add the ginger/garlic paste and sauté for a minute or two.

Blend all the spices except the garam masala and the crushed peppercorns with the reserved boiled water and pour this into the pan. As the liquid reduces, blend the garam masala, crushed pepper and the lime juice into the cream and add. As soon as you see it thicken slightly, add the vegetables, check the seasoning and add the fresh coriander.

Remove from the heat. Serve as a main dish with parathas or as an accompaniment.

'Vigna 'nt 'l sas, ort an 'l gras'

VINES IN STONY SOIL AND VEG IN RICH

Cauliflower growing tips

Sow 1 cm deep in trays from May to July. Harvest times vary greatly depending on the variety.

Verde di Macerata: An early green variety, which can also be sown in January for an early harvest. It forms a medium-sized head, and when sown between May and July is harvested until the end of December.

Verona Tardivo: This is a late variety, snow white, and harvested from March to the end of April.

Romanesco: This is the classic, green, spiralling variety that is now beginning to appear in good greengrocers in the UK. They have small heads and each floret spirals into a point. This variety is harvested until the end of January.

Di Jesi: Early. Creamy white-coloured head, with white spiralling florets, though not as pronounced as the Romanesco. Harvest until the end of December.

Palla di Neve sel Adige: An early variety from the Dolomites that forms medium-sized 'snowball' white heads. Harvest from September to the end of November.

Marzatico: This is a Neapolitan variety with a large head and tall habit. The head is large and ice white and resistant to low temperatures. Harvest until the end of March.

Kale Young kale leaves can be eaten raw, but kale is an excellent cooking vegetable. There is only one kale worth its salt. Though commonly called Cavolo Nero, its proper name is Cavolo Lacinato Nero di Toscana. I think it is the best kale in the world. It is superb pan-fried with a little bacon and garlic and is also used to make the national dish of Florence, Ribollita Toscana. Ribollita means re-boiled, and this was originally a stew of borlotti beans and a ham hock made the day before and heated up on the day. It's a peasant dish, but you try and buy some in Florence and I can assure you that you won't pay peasant prices!

RIBOLLITA by Giancarlo and Katie Caldesi

One of the most popular soups in Tuscany, this version uses a roughly chopped, rustic soffritto. It is a classic peasant recipe. SERVES 6

200 ml olive oil
2 cloves of garlic, 1 chopped
100 g white onions, roughly chopped
300 g carrots, roughly chopped
300 g celery, roughly chopped
400 g courgettes, roughly chopped
300 g Savoy cabbage, roughly chopped
300 g black kale (Cavolo Nero), roughly chopped
200 g spinach, chopped

550 g potatoes, roughly chopped
100 g tomatoes, peeled and chopped
800 g cooked cannellini beans or 2 x 400 g cans
1 litre vegetable stock
1 white farmhouse loaf
extra-virgin olive oil, for drizzling
salt and freshly ground black pepper
freshly grated Pecorino cheese, to serve

HEAT THE OLIVE OIL IN A LARGE PAN and add the chopped garlic and onions. Cook gently until the onions are soft. Add the carrots and celery, and season. Cook over a low heat for a further 15 minutes until this soffritto turns golden, stirring occasionally. Once the soffritto is ready, add the courgettes, Savoy cabbage, black kale and spinach. Leave to sweat for about 10 minutes, then add the potatoes and tomatoes. Mash half the cannellini beans and stir into the pan. Cook gently for about 5 minutes. Add the stock and simmer, covered, for 30 minutes, stirring regularly. About 10 minutes before the end of cooking, add the remaining cannellini beans.

Cut the bread into slices and toast them in the oven at Gas Mark 3/170°C (or use the grill or a toaster). Rub each slice with the whole garlic clove and drizzle with a little extra-virgin olive oil. Place a layer of toast in the bottom of a shallow ovenproof lasagne dish and pour over some of the soup. Repeat until all the toast and soup have been used.

Let the soup stand for a while before serving. Alternatively, the soup can be kept warm, uncovered, in the oven for up to 15 minutes. If you put the ribollita in the oven, make sure all the toast is covered by the soup or it will burn. Serve in warm bowls, drizzled with extra-virgin olive oil and scattered with Pecorino.

Cima di Rapa Go to any Italian restaurant in the US and you'll get broccoli raab, served blanched and then seared. Its traditional use is for a pasta dish from Puglia called Orecchiette e Cima di Rape. Many pasta shapes have a particular sauce associated with them, and orecchiette are only used with this vegetable and this sauce.

This vegetable does have an identity crisis here, though it's beginning to find its way into markets and greengrocers. Literally, cima di rapa means 'turnip tops'. It's also called broccoli raab (or rabe). In Britain we sometimes call it tender sprouting broccoli or sprouting broccoli, but while similar to this it's just not quite the same.

Orecchiette e Cima di Rape
ORECCHIETTE PASTA WITH BROCCOLI RAAB

From Puglia in the south of Italy, typical of the cooking from this region, one of the tastiest pasta dishes and a favourite of our household. You can preserve any excess cima di rapa by making the famous sauce and putting it in hermetically sealed jars. These will keep for up to a year in your larder. SERVES 4

400 g cima di rapa/broccoli raab, roughly chopped
4–5 tablespoons olive oil
1 red onion, sliced
2 cloves of garlic, sliced
3 anchovies, roughly chopped
1 glass white wine

500 g orecchiette pasta
butter
freshly grated Pecorino or Parmesan cheese
chilli oil
salt and freshly ground black pepper

COOK THE CIMA DI RAPA in slightly salted water. Drain through a sieve, reserving the water for cooking the pasta later.

Pour the oil into a pan and gently sauté the sliced onion and garlic with the anchovies. Turn up the heat so that the onions start to sizzle and then pour in the white wine. Add the cima di rapa and mix well, adding a drizzle more oil if the mixture looks dry. Lower the heat to allow the flavours to mix and keep warm on a low flame until ready to serve over the pasta.

Meanwhile, bring the reserved water to the boil, cook the pasta according to the instructions on the packet, drain, stir in a knob of butter and then add the sauce. Grate some Pecorino on top and season with chilli oil and freshly ground black pepper.

Cima di Rapa growing tips

There is a 40 Day variety that is ready to eat just 40 days after sowing (and sometimes after only 35 days). There are 60 Day, 90 Day and 120 Day varieties too. The general rule is that the longer growing the variety, the better the quality. The 40 and 60 Day varieties can be sown every month for five months, from about April to the end of August, and five crops per year is not bad. These two varieties grow so quickly, they should be harvested as soon as they look like the picture on the packet.

Cima di Rapa 40: Very early. The quickest variety, from seed to plate in 40 days. Sow from March to September and harvest as soon as it is ready.

Cima di Rapa 60: Mid/early. Ready to eat 60 days from sowing. Sow from March to September. Slightly slower to bolt than the 40 Day variety but should still be harvested as soon as it is ready and placed in the fridge. Cima di Rapa 90 is a much better-quality variety, but it takes three months from seed to be ready to eat. Sow from March to July.

Cima di Rapa 120: Late. Whereas with the 40 and 60 Day varieties you can stagger the sowing for a continuous harvest, the 120 variety is sown from July to August and harvested from November to March. The plant will encounter cold weather, but is hardy.

Cima di Rapa Maceratese: Mid/early. An upright plant that is easy to grow. It doesn't produce florets and has long, slightly serrated, tasty leaves that are used in pasta and soups. Sow from April to August and harvest until the end of the summer.

Rapa da Foglia Senza Testa: Early. It translates as 'leaf turnip without bulb', and you get exactly what it says on the tin. It is an upright but open plant with large, long green leaves that have a mild brassica flavour. When cooked, they are tender and tasty and are often used with pasta. Sow from April until September.

Turnips Some vegetables come in and out of fashion, but turnips never seem to be one of them, languishing as they do with a fairly unattractive gastronomic image. But they are not that bad and, when cooked simply, fried with some garlic, properly seasoned and then drizzled with a good olive oil upon serving, they are not bad at all.

Rapa con Mele e Salame
TURNIPS WITH APPLES AND SALAMI

My nonna used to make this dish and it's typical of the alpine Biellese region of Piedmont. Turnips are not the most glamorous of vegetables but this is a surprisingly good dish. The turnips were harvested with the apples after the pigs had been killed and salami and sausages made. The sweetness of the apples balances the strong turnip flavour and like many peasant dishes, it is simple, cheap and tasty. SERVES 4

150 g piece of salami
1 kg turnips, sliced

4 eating apples, peeled and sliced
salt and freshly ground black pepper

DICE THE SALAMI and fry it in a little oil. When cooked, remove it from the pan and add the sliced turnips and apples to the same pan. Season. Cook slowly for at least 40 minutes then return the salami to the pan. Either serve with polenta or put into preserving jars and boil the jars for 10 minutes to hermetically seal them. This way, the contents will last for about a year in the larder and, like a Christmas pudding, the flavour will improve with age.

Turnips growing tips

Turnips are usually sown from May to the end of July and harvested from July until about November, depending on where you are. Sow them 1 cm deep directly into the ground, leaving 10 cm between the rows. Even stony ground is fine for growing turnips.

Di Milano a Colletto Rosa: Early variety, flat with a good-sized bulb. Classic red collar and white base with pure white flesh. Sow from April to the end of July.

Viola: This variety has a purple collar and a month shorter sowing season than the Milano. The flavour is slightly stronger, but it is sweet and meaty. Sow from May to July.

Bianca di Lodi (Lodigiana): Mid/early white variety from northern Italy, near Milan. It produces a good-sized bulb. Harvest from September to the end of November.

cipolle,

aglio e porri

ONIONS, GARLIC AND LEEKS

I associate pickling onions with a classic British ploughman's, large white onions with Spain and golden onions with France. But I always associate red onions with Italy.

Garlic is associated with France more than Italy, yet it is heavily used in every region of the country and in a great many dishes. Leeks, also, are associated more closely with Wales than with Italy, but are neverthless part of our cuisine. The Latin name for leeks is _Allium porrum_. Allium means onion and the Italian for leek is 'porro' still. Of course leeks have that onion flavour but they are not as strong as onion, which makes them very versatile in the kitchen.

Onions Onions are often a background flavour, yet raw onions go so well with certain foods such as cheeses, especially strong ones like Provolone piccante or Cheddar (a marriage made in heaven), but not so well with blue cheeses or milder cheeses. But cook an onion and it now goes well with blue cheese in a red onion tart, or with Gorgonzola and walnuts. Similarly cook onion in a flan or quiche with softer, milder cheeses or on pizza with mozzarella. Red onions have a high sugar content, so are excellent raw in salads and, when cooked, caramelize well.

Cipolle Ripiene della Nonna Angela
NONNA ANGELA'S STUFFED ONIONS

I still dream of my nonna's stuffed onions: really simple, really tasty. It's one of those recipes where you throw everything into a bowl, mix it together then use as a stuffing. The precise quantities depend on how many onion shells you have and how large they are, but the basic proportions should be as here. The general rule is that you need about twice as much raw meat as dry ingredients. The amount of egg for binding depends on how 'wet' your meat is. SERVES 4

4 large white onions
200 g minced veal or pork
50 g Italian sausage, chopped
20 g parsley, chopped
2 tablespoons grated Parmesan cheese

1 fresh bread roll, grated into crumbs
1 egg
a drizzle of olive oil
salt and freshly ground black pepper

CUT THE TOP AND BOTTOM OFF THE ONIONS, cut in half through the middle and separate the rings – it doesn't matter if they have holes at the bottom as the stuffing (ripieno) is fairly stiff and won't fall out. If the walls of the onion are not that thick, then use two onion shells inside each other as this not only holds the ripieno, but also intensifies the main flavour.

Put the remaining ingredients in a bowl, season well, and mix together until you have a paste that is pliable. Spoon this mixture evenly into the onion segments.

Place on a baking tray and bake at Gas Mark 5/190°C for about 10 minutes, or until the filling is cooked through and the meat is starting to crisp on top, but make sure the onions don't burn.

Remember the onions will be of varying sizes, so make sure you check the largest ones to see they are cooked through. My method is to prepare an extra onion to eat – sorry, I mean to check straight away – just to make sure they are definitely cooked. It's my excuse and I'm sticking to it.

These are delicious cold, but to reheat prior to serving, place in a medium hot oven for about 5 minutes. Grate some additional Parmesan cheese on top just before serving.

Baccalà con Cipolle, Crema e Polenta

SALT COD WITH ONIONS, CREAM AND POLENTA

Dad always made this at Christmas with any baccalà (salt cod) he hadn't sold in the deli. He always hoped he wouldn't sell it all as this dish reminded him of his mother, and the recipe continues to be made in the same way two generations later. No one much liked it at home except Dad and me, so it is quite a special dish for me too. My mother-in-law cooks baccalà in a tomato sauce, and while excellent this way just reminds me of Dad.

Baccalà is cod that has been preserved by salting and is certainly not a new thing. It's well known in the Caribbean where British ships would carry salt cod, and also in Portugal and its colonies such as Brazil, where it is called baccalao.

In Italy, different regions favour different sizes and shapes and thicknesses of baccalà. I saw a documentary on it once and it was so confusing that I took none of it in. Suffice to say that in Britain you can usually only get good baccalà from an Italian deli at Christmas, or from Portuguese or West Indian shops.

Baccalà is really hard and tough. We used to cut it in the shop with a hacksaw. Try and buy it in manageable pieces that will fit into a bowl for soaking. Otherwise you might end up trying to cut it with the rusty saw from your tool box!

This isn't a dish you can do at the last minute, you need to prepare the fish the day before – but it is worth it as it's really tasty.

400 g baccalà (salt cod)	*2 golden onions, sliced*
milk	*1 tablespoon capers in vinegar, drained*
1 bay leaf	*500 ml double cream*
flour	*freshly ground black pepper*
olive oil	*'instant' polenta to serve*

THE MORNING BEFORE REQUIRED, wash the fish in slowly running water for 10 minutes and then put it to soak, first in water, changing the water at least once, and then to soak overnight in the fridge, this time in milk with a bay leaf. Make sure the fish is covered – a sealable container is ideal.

The next day, take the fish from the milk and cut into large cubes, removing any bones you find. Dust the pieces of fish with flour and fry in hot olive oil until lightly browned, then remove. Fry the onion until golden, then turn down the heat and return the fish to the pan. Add the capers, season with black pepper and pour in the double cream, allowing the dish to slowly heat through and the flavours to mix while you prepare the polenta according to the instructions on the packet.

This dish could be served with good crusty 'campagnolo' bread or potatoes instead of polenta, but not with rice, which will simply absorb all the cream sauce.

SARDINES IN SAOR

This is a Venetian dish, which I tasted first in Piedmont. There are a lot of Venetian women in the area who came from the Veneto region to work as mondine in the rice fields, up to their knees in water every day harvesting rice. It was a hard job, but the girls were given basic lodgings in a dorm all together and given food and some money and were also paid in rice. This work was seasonal and the young girls were able to go back home with some savings and quite a bit of rice. Some of them even worked with babies on their backs in slings and many of them stayed, married local boys and set up home. So it's not unusual to eat Venetian dishes in Piedmont.

This recipe was given to me by Bianella and Pier Piscina (parents of my friend Jacopo). They are quite a typical Piedmontese family, in that Pier was born and bred in Paris of Piedmontese parents. There is a massive French/Swiss influence in Piedmont and much coming and going between. Turin was the capital of the Savoy region and most Piedmontese speak French. My father was the only child in the family not born in France; my grandmother would sometimes speak to me in French and I would always reply in Italian. Pier is married to Bianella, who is Venetian. The thing I love most about this recipe is Bianella's attention to detail and clear respect for the dish. SERVES 6

1 kg fresh sardines   *500 ml red wine vinegar*
1 kg white onions (Musona)   *flour*
sunflower oil for frying   *salt and freshly ground black pepper*

CUT THE FISH with a paring knife and scrape them from the tails to the heads. Wash the sardines carefully and then remove their heads. Gut the fish, taking care to empty the innards. Flatten them on a chopping board and cut the tail fin off but leave the tail whole. Wash the fish again carefully, place on kitchen paper and leave them for at least 30 minutes to completely dry.

Meanwhile, prepare the saor. Finely slice the onions into rings and place in a flameproof dish with oil to just cover the bottom. Cook them on a low heat, making sure they don't brown. As soon as they are soft, pour in 400 ml vinegar and season. Continue to heat on a low flame until the vinegar has been absorbed into the onions. Remove from the heat, cover and put aside.

Coat each sardine in flour. Heat some sunflower oil in a frying pan and fry the fish a few at a time. Remove with a spatula, put them to drain on kitchen paper and sprinkle with a little salt. When both the fish and the saor are cold, place them in a terrine in layers with a thin layer of onion in between the fish. One third of the saor onions should be used on top to cover the fish completely. Finally, douse the whole with another 100 ml of vinegar. Cover with cling film and place the terrine in a cool place, but not in the fridge, for 2–3 days.

To present: Saor should be served cold in the same container, with hot white polenta (or yellow if unavailable). In Venice, it is said that you should savour the Saor, eating them over a number of days. Many say that the flavour improves with time.

Onion growing tips

Onions can be sown very easily from seed and the benefit of doing this is the value for money, as in one pack you can get about 1,400 seeds – a huge saving compared to the cost of onion sets, although these will produce more quickly of course. Generally you sow in spring for the same year and in autumn for an early crop the next.

The simplest way to grow onions from seed is just to sprinkle some seeds into a container or seed tray, 1 cm down, and a chive-like shoot will grow. Scoop these out with your little finger and transplant into the ground 5 cm apart. They don't mind the cold and will grow on and swell with watering (onions have a high water content).

When you pull your onions (you'll know when they are ready as the stalks will go brown and half the onion will be sticking out of the ground), roughly clean without washing, and leave them in the sun all day to dry off a bit. You can use the dried necks to plait your onions together. If you don't know how, ask any girl (I'm not being sexist, I promise: this has proved true for every female questioned so far, but not for the gents!).

Red onions generally store quite well, in a shady, cool (room temperature, but avoid the kitchen) and airy place. It's not good to keep them in a conservatory or porch, as these can get hot during the day and freezing at night. Golden onions store the best and can last months once the outer skin has dried out.

As I manage a specialist seed-producing company with many regional and local varieties, I have decided not to cover onion sets, which are usually not regional anyway and are very straightforward to sow and grow. Some popular varieties would be Red Baron (red), Snow Ball (white) and Stoccarda/Stuttgarter Reisen (golden), and I would recommend all three for their reliability and good characteristics.

RED ONIONS

Rossa Lunga di Firenze: Long red onion from Florence that is so regional it's not even found in some other parts of Tuscany. It looks like a shallot and is a good-sized onion with sweet flesh. Very good raw. The high sugar content means that it is particularly sweet. A past RHS Award of Garden Merit winner. Sow from February to May.

Tondo Rossa di Toscana: Much more widely available in Tuscany, this is a round variety. It is reliable in both growing habit and flavour and is also a good storer. It is preferred for cooking although, as mentioned, all red onions are good raw because of their sweetness.

Rossa di Genova/Bassano: The classic Italian red onion. Squashed or flattened at its poles, large, juicy and sweet with a beautiful deep red papery jacket, and really versatile. I'm unsure why it's called a 'Genova (Bassano)' onion, as Genova and Bassano are about 500 kilometres apart, but I suspect it's grown in both areas. Sow in spring and autumn.

Rossa di Savona: This regional onion is translucent, round and, due to its great characteristics, favoured for eating raw. It is a good-sized variety that stores well. Sow spring and autumn.

Tropea Rossa: Possibly the most famous and highest-quality red onion in Italy. A broadsheet newspaper once published an article that claimed that the Tropea onion might be one of the ingredients in Viagra! Our sales went through the roof. It is so sweet you can practically eat it like an apple – and it makes a wonderful onion paste that you can use in pasta, on bruschetta and in numerous other dishes. It stores well too, making it, in my opinion, the most gastronomic of all varieties. There is also a Long Red Tropea onion, which is less well known. Sow in spring and autumn.

GOLDEN AND WHITE ONIONS

Borrettana: Famous small, flat 'cipolline' pickling onion with sweet white flesh and an unusually high sugar content. A very good variety that can be used fresh as small button onions in stews and casseroles. Sow only in autumn.

Dorata di Parma: 'Golden of Parma'. Mid/late. Large round golden bulb with white flesh. A good storer that goes especially well with other ingredients from Parma, such as Parmesan cheese and Parma ham. Sow from March to May and July to September.

Salad Onion Giugnese: A medium-sized Italian salad onion with a semi-flat bulb and pure white flesh. Tender and tasty – ideal for eating raw. Sow in spring and autumn.

Musona Tondo Bianca: A white Spanish-style cooking onion. Good-sized bulb. Sow from February to March and from July to August.

Piatta di Bergamo: This variety comes from the home of Franchi seeds and is a flat golden onion of good dimensions. The flesh is white and it is a good storer. Sow February to March.

Ramata di Milano: A very large golden onion with white flesh from fashionable Milan. It is neither round nor long, but egg-shaped. Stores well. Sow from February to March.

Valencia Tardiva: A late variety from the eastern part of Spain, where some of the best onions come from. A good variety both for cooking and for eating with Spanish hams and cheeses.

Spanish Onion Valenciana Temprana: A classic onion of Valencia. An early medium-sized variety producing large spinning-top-shaped onions with golden skin, thick, tender flesh and a mild flavour. This variety is a moderate storer but does have excellent flavour characteristics.

Salad Onion Barletta: Small round 'cipolline' white salad onion (pearl onion) that is suitable for pickling. Sow from February to March.

Spring Onion Cipollotti a Mazzo: Long white stems used for salads and oriental cooking. Sow this fast grower from February to end of July in succession for a longer cropping period.

Garlic The easiest way to peel garlic is to bash a clove with the heel of a knife and the skin will just come off. Some chefs will sprinkle some salt on the chopping board, which helps hold the garlic in place when you bash it, and some say this makes it creamier and less strong.

Garlic needs cold to grow, so don't store it in the fridge – it will think it is in season and start to sprout!

Spaghetti Aglio, Olio e Peperoncino
SPAGHETTI WITH GARLIC, OLIVE OIL AND CHILLI

Aglio, Olio e Peperoncino is one of those classic dishes that you eat at two in the morning after a night out, as it's quick and easy to make and most people have garlic, oil and chilli in the cupboard. Dried, powdered chilli works best with this dish because you want the heat to be even, not like Chinese chilli beef where one mouthful is hot and the next is not. Different chilli powders can have completely different strengths so some trial and error may be involved. Add less rather than more if unsure. SERVES 4

500 g spaghetti
a good bunch of fresh parsley
8 tablespoons extra-virgin olive oil

3 cloves of garlic, sliced
dried chilli flakes or chilli powder, to taste
grated Parmesan cheese, to serve

BRING SOME SALTED WATER TO THE BOIL and start the pasta cooking.

Meanwhile, wash and chop the parsley. Heat the oil in a saucepan and gently soften the garlic and chilli in the oil until it only just starts to colour. At that point, add 2 tablespoons of water and let it simmer for a minute before removing from the heat.

Strain the pasta and dress with the oil mixture, adding the parsley only at the last minute. Serve with Parmesan cheese to taste and a cold white wine.

L'aj a l'e' le spesiari d'I paisan'

GARLIC IS THE PHARMACY OF THE COUNTRY MAN

Garlic growing tips

Garlic needs cold, and preferably a spell of sub-zero temperatures, for it to really prosper. That's why you plant it in the winter from November to March (I do two sowings, one in November and the other in February). There are arguments over whether pre- or post-Christmas-planted garlic is better, but I think the garlic that is planted before Christmas, preferably in November, does have the edge. That said, I still plant some garlic later so that I have a regular supply.

To grow garlic, you separate the cloves from the heads (but keep their jackets on – don't undress them); each clove will make a head. It is best to dig the soil to make sure it is friable. It is a bulb that will have to swell, and if the soil is heavy clay that's going to make things difficult. Separate the heads into cloves and plant these 5 cm deep with 8 cm between the rows. Before you harvest the garlic in late spring or early summer, dig around one to check that it is well developed. Other indications of ripeness are that the growing shoot may fall over or the plant starts looking sad and feeble. It's best to pull the whole thing up, growing shoot with garlic bulb attached, then, providing it's a warm, dry day, leave the garlic outside on the earth to start the process of drying. You can then bring them indoors at the end of the day and hang them in a dry airy room. You can plait the garlic if you wish at this point. It should keep for some months before it starts to hollow out.

Garlic, of course, has a strong flavour, but some garlics, the red ones in particular, are sweeter and there are subtle differences between the different varieties. There are many different domestic and European varieties, but these are the ones that I know on a day-to-day basis. There are some superb British garlic companies and the one I would recommend is The Garlic Farm on the Isle of Wight.

Rosso di Sulmona: This particular hard-neck variety comes from the south of Italy, from the Abruzzo region, which gets surprisingly cold in the winter. It is a red garlic, sweeter than white and not as strong. It suits dishes where the sweetness and mildness complement the flavour.

Bianco Veneto: This variety is called white Venetian but is also well known and grown in Piacenza. It is a typical garlic, medium-sized with a soft neck, and a good reliable variety.

French: There are white and red French varieties and these are the ones that we are most used to eating and growing in the UK. They are also larger than the Italian varieties. With some vegetables, the larger they are, the weaker the flavour, but not in the case of French garlic, which has excellent quality and flavour characteristics.

Spanish: Spanish garlic is, to generalize, average in terms of quality. It is of a good overall standard and in size comes between the small Italian and large French garlics. It also nicely fills the gap in the periods when the other garlics are in short supply.

Elefant: This is a very large garlic that in fact is not a head of cloves at all, but one giant clove. It has become very popular in recent years in the UK.

Leeks Francesco da Mosto makes a lovely leek risotto and The River Cafe has a leek and bacon tart, but leek is usually an ingredient rather than the star of the show in any dish.

Leeks, like onions, go very well with cheese, potatoes and smoked meats like pancetta, bacon and speck. They are best simply roasted or fried together with these other ingredients.

PORRI AL MONTASIO by Country House Montali

The sweetness of leeks combines well with the sour taste of Montasio cheese. SERVES 4

675 g leeks, white and yellow parts only
2 tablespoons butter
3 tablespoons flour
450 ml milk

150 g Montasio or Cheddar cheese, cut into 1 cm
cubes
salt, pepper and nutmeg to taste

CLEAN THE LEEKS and cut each into three equal pieces. Halve each cylinder crosswise on a bias. Cook in lightly salted boiling water for three minutes and set aside. In a separate saucepan, melt the butter and add the flour. Stir until the roux is golden brown and add a quarter of the milk, stirring until smooth. Add the remaining milk and cook until thickened, approximately 3 minutes. Stir two thirds of the cheese into the sauce until melted. Season with salt, pepper and nutmeg.

Butter the bottom of a 20 x 20 cm ceramic plate. Stand the leeks bias-side up and drizzle with the sauce. Top with the remaining cheese and bake at Gas Mark 4/180°C for 10 minutes or until the cheese is bubbly and golden brown. Serve hot.

Leek growing tips

Sow leeks 1 cm deep from March to May, allowing 5 cm between each plant. They are good winter-harvesting plants, only needing an air temperature of 10°C once planted.

Gigante d'Inverno: Literally 'Winter Giant', this large, white variety has excellent resistance to the cold, so you can harvest it until the end of February.

Carentan: Carentan is a superb French leek, which is a late, medium-sized variety. It is resistant to low temperatures.

Tornado F1: A late, professional variety that is ideally suited to autumn and winter harvest and can be harvested during December. A large leek with a long white leg and good resistance to low temperatures.

fagioli,

piselli e mais

BEANS, PEAS AND CORN

_There are beans where you eat the whole pod and beans that you shell,
and both are equally delicious for different reasons._

I won't talk about runner beans here. Not because I don't like them, but because I have little experience of them as they really don't exist much outside the UK, apart from places with ex-pat communities such as Australia and the south of Spain.

The pea has to be one of the most popular vegetables in Britain. Offer children sausages with celeriac, pumpkin, courgettes or peas, and you know which one they'll choose. And where would a pub order of steak and chips be without a side of peas, for example?

You might not associate corn with Italy, but it is the staple food of northern Italy, where the corn is dried and ground down to make polenta.

Shelling Beans

Borlotti Beans Often called by the singular 'borlotto' in Italian, this speckled shelling bean is used widely all over Italy. They are hearty flavoursome beans that will fill you up – meaty without being meat.

Cannellini Beans These small, white, kidney-shaped beans are very similar to the French flageolet beans that are used in cassoulet. This is also made in the parts of Italy that border France and Switzerland, but with cannellini beans instead. They are super quality beans and indispensable in winter dishes. They give good texture to stews, soups and casseroles and have a good flavour, even after being dried and rehydrated in water overnight.

Lupini Beans A favourite of Puglia in particular, these are most often eaten in bars with beer! The bean is yellowish and flat but fairly meaty nonetheless. They are boiled in salted water and have a clear 'jacket' that surrounds them. You squeeze them and they pop out of their skins, straight into your mouth, and are washed down with the beer. Beer and beans – maybe not the ideal combination to combat the hole in the ozone layer, but they are full of fibre and far healthier than crisps.

Fagioli di Spagna Fagioli di Spagna are white or cream-coloured large butter beans, which are really popular in Italy. You can buy them in tins along with borlotti and cannellini beans and they have a floury texture that melts in the mouth. They are excellent cooked and made into a bean salad, with tuna and peppers for example, but are used extensively in hot dishes too.

Lima Beans These are not native to Italy and are not used that much. They are large, flat, cream and red shelling beans that have been cultivated in Peru for thousands of years. You should always boil them as they contain low levels of cyanide, which is released by the cooking process (although the European varieties have very low levels compared to some others around the world). Hope that hasn't put you off as they have a lovely creamy texture and a good buttery, sweet flavour.

Lentils Lentils are most often associated with France but are widely used in Italian cooking too, especially at New Year, when they are served with a cooking salami called cottechino or with

zampone (pigs' trotters). It's said that for each one you eat, you will become richer. So everyone always eats loads of them. They are really high in fibre and can be big or small, brown, yellow, green, orange or black; some you soak first and others you don't. I always think the small ones are the best in terms of flavour, plus you get more on a fork on your New Year's money quest!

Broad Beans The Latin name for broad beans is *Vicia faba*, and they are still called 'fava' in Italian. They are really important in southern Italy where they are used commonly, although one problem is 'favismo', a genetic allergy to broad beans found in Sicily and Sardinia in particular but in southern Italy in general, which can prove fatal. They are full of vitamins, protein, fibre and mineral salts and aid the urinary function. They are very low in calories and fat but they are high in natural salts. Dried broad beans actually have more protein content. They are a delicious vegetable anyway, being eaten both cooked and raw. I have eaten a lovely snack of sliced broad beans that were deep-fried (like crisps) and then salted and served with an aperitif. I have a Sicilian friend called Matteo who is a barber in Luton and he is crazy about them. He also makes the best pasta with broad beans that I have ever tasted – his recipe can be found on page 108.

Lenticchie con Piselli e Pancetta
LENTILS WITH PEAS AND PANCETTA

This is a favourite dish of mine. Simple, tasty, filling, quick and a good accompaniment to meat dishes. Canned peas actually work better for this dish than fresh, just as canned tomatoes sometimes work better than fresh for certain sauces. A stock cube also works well because it's quite salty and, along with the pancetta or bacon, will really lift the lentils and give them a good flavour. If you've got some good home-made stock though, use that, and adjust the seasoning accordingly as it won't be as salty as a dado (stock cube). SERVES 4

olive oil

100 g pancetta, speck or smoked bacon, roughly cut
    into strips

1 medium onion (Ramata di Milano), chopped

2 whole cloves of garlic, peeled

500 g lentils, soaked if necessary

400 ml stock, made from a stock cube

1 small can peas

salt and freshly ground black pepper

ADD A SLOSH OF OLIVE OIL to a frying pan and start to pan-fry the pancetta or bacon for a minute over a medium heat before adding the onion and the garlic to soften. Don't overcrowd the pan with the bacon as all the juices will come out and you'll be boiling it instead of frying it – we want the bacon to impart its wonderful flavour to the oil.

When the onion has softened, add the lentils and the stock and reduce to a simmer. Cover and cook the lentils for the amount of time indicated on the package, stirring occasionally but not too vigorously as you don't want to squash them. Don't be scared of adding more water, especially towards the end of cooking.

Check the seasoning. The pancetta will be salty, but do make sure the dish is properly seasoned with salt and pepper. When ready, the lentils should have soaked up the liquid but should still be moist and loose, not dry and sticky. Stir in the peas and quickly heat through. As you serve them, add a filo (drizzle) of good olive oil.

Insalata di Borlotti e Tonno

BEAN AND TUNA SALAD

A simple summer dish you can make the day before. It's a good picnic dish or an excellent mixture for stuffed tomatoes, and lovely as a light summer lunch with a glass of wine. The recipe works very well with either canned or fresh borlotti. SERVES 4 AS A STARTER OR SIDE DISH

250 g fresh borlotti beans, boiled until tender, or
  1 can borlotti beans, drained
1 can tuna fish in olive oil
1 red onion (Tropea), sliced

lemon juice
a sprig of fresh parsley, chopped
salt and freshly ground black pepper

PLACE THE BEANS AND THE TUNA WITH ALL ITS OIL INTO A BOWL. Add the onion slices and a squeeze of lemon juice, avoiding any pips by passing the juice through your fingers. Season with pepper and a little salt and stir in the chopped parsley. That is it. Now enjoy summer on a plate!

Pasta e Fagioli

PASTA AND BEANS

This is a classic Venetian recipe. The bean to use is a borlotti called Lamon, but Lingua di Fuoco or Borlotti from Vigevano could also be used. I have suggested two different shapes of pasta. The round, short ditaloni is what I am used to for Pasta e Fagioli. However, they are difficult to find in England, so tagliatelle or even broken spaghetti are also acceptable. SERVES 4–6

120 g belly of pork or piece of ham
400 g fresh borlotti beans (Lamon)
1 onion (Musona)
1 carrot (Nantese of Chioggia)
1 head of celery (Dorato d'Asti)

scraped Parmesan crusts
500 g ditaloni or tagliatelle
olive oil
salt and freshly ground black pepper

WASH AND SCRAPE THE PORK. Immerse in boiling water for a few minutes. Put with all the other ingredients except the pasta and olive oil in a heavy saucepan and cover with salted water. Place on the hob and simmer for about 30 minutes until the beans are tender. Remove about half the beans with a slotted spoon, purée them and set aside. Add the pasta to the saucepan. When the pasta is cooked, return the puréed beans to the pan and stir in. Remove the meat, vegetables and Parmesan crusts from the pan and cut them all into four portions. Serve the soup in bowls, topped with a piece of meat and a piece of Parmesan crust. Drizzle a really good-quality olive oil on top just before serving, accompanied with a large rustic loaf.

Insalata Aromatica di Cannellini

AROMATIC CANNELLINI BEAN SALAD

Cannellini beans tend to be used in hot dishes more than anything else and so here is something a little different – a salad recipe. SERVES 4

130 g cannellini beans
1 bay leaf
1 ripe tomato
1 medium onion
50 g sweet black olives

1 clove of garlic
a bunch of basil
2 tablespoons extra-virgin olive oil
1 teaspoon white wine vinegar
salt and freshly ground black pepper

IF USING DRIED BEANS, SOAK FIRST FOR 12 HOURS before cooking as for fresh beans. If using fresh, rinse, place in a saucepan and cover with cold water, adding the bay leaf, and boil for an hour. Remove from the heat when cooked and allow to cool, discarding the bay leaf.

Meanwhile, deseed the tomato and dice the pulp. Chop the onion, olives, garlic and basil and add to the cold cannellini beans in a salad bowl.

Make a vinaigrette with the oil, vinegar, salt and pepper, and dress the salad.

BROAD BEAN PURÉE from Country House Montali

SERVES 6 AS A SIDE DISH

60 g dried broad beans, rinsed
½ carrot, halved lengthwise
2 cloves of garlic
½ onion, quartered
1 sprig of parsley

2 tablespoons extra-virgin oil
salt to taste
350 ml water
1 tablespoon lemon juice
1 tablespoon tahini

COMBINE THE BEANS, carrot, 1 whole garlic clove, onion, parsley, 1 tablespoon olive oil, salt and water in a large pot and cook over a low heat for 40 minutes or until the beans are tender.

Remove the beans and purée them in a blender. Discard the other used ingredients. Add the remaining olive oil, garlic, lemon juice and tahini and purée again. Season to taste.

PANISCIA FROM BURONZO

This is a peasant winter dish made with ingredients dried or preserved for the long winter months. The salami traditionally used was most probably 'd'la duja', which is a salami from Piedmont that is preserved for the bitter winter months in barrels of lard. The salami was wiped clean of the lard before using, but the lard was kept for frying and was quite flavoursome. Paniscia is rather more liquid than a risotto. SERVES 4

100 g piece of gammon, chopped
200 g borlotti beans, fresh or dried and soaked
2 celery sticks, chopped
1 large carrot, chopped
1 leek, chopped
150 g Savoy cabbage, chopped
a few ripe tomatoes, peeled, deseeded and chopped
1 onion, chopped

60 g pancetta or smoked bacon, chopped
60 g butter
½ cooking salami, skinned and broken into pieces
1 glass red wine
350 g risotto rice (Sant' Andrea, carnaroli or baldo)
salt and freshly ground black pepper
grated Parmesan cheese to serve

PLACE THE GAMMON AND THE borlotti in a large saucepan, cover with water, and boil for 1 hour. Add the celery, carrot, leek and cabbage, together with the tomatoes and salt and pepper. Boil for a further hour.

In a pan (traditionally a terracotta pan), gently fry the onion and pancetta in the butter. Add the salami and the red wine and fry until slightly evaporated. Add the rice and cook as for a risotto, adding the broth from the beans a little at a time. Add the vegetables and the gammon cut into chunks and cook for approximately 20–25 minutes. Serve in a bowl, sprinkled with Parmesan.

Pasta con Fave

BROAD BEAN PASTA

This recipe has been given by two family friends, Matteo and Barbara from Luton, yet another area with a big Italian presence. Bedford has the largest population of Italians in the UK – one person in every seven; they were drawn there by the great brick works that dominated the town for years. Matteo is Sicilian by birth and a barber by trade, but both he and Barbara love to cook – especially for others – and of course it goes without saying that they love to eat, especially if it includes something fresh from the garden. A simple dish to prepare, I don't think you will believe how good this tastes. You need a short pasta for this recipe, so spaghetti and linguine are out.
SERVES 2

50–70 g butter
1 tablespoon olive oil
½ onion, chopped small
2 cloves of garlic, crushed

250–300 g small broad beans
150 g small ditaloni pasta (or according to taste)
salt and freshly ground black pepper
grated Parmesan or Pecorino cheese to serve

MELT THE BUTTER WITH THE OIL and fry the onion until softened. Add the garlic and soften slightly (taking care not to burn it), then add the broad beans with ½ cup water, salt and pepper.

Bring to the boil, cover and simmer until cooked.

For the pasta, boil a saucepan of water, add salt and cook until the pasta is al dente. Drain, leaving a little liquid in the pan. Mix together the pasta, reserved cooking liquid and beans. Serve topped with grated Parmesan or Pecorino cheese.

'al frigo e' nemmico del formaggio'

THE FRIDGE IS THE ENEMY OF CHEESE

Bean growing tips

Beans are part of the *Leguminosae* family and are really easy to grow – making them a popular choice for children to grow at school. Beans fix nitrogen into the soil and take part of their food from the ground and part from the air. This means you can sow them close together and, as they also grow upwards, they are the ultimate space-saving veggie. They are especially good in pots and containers. You don't need to feed beans as you would tomatoes.

BORLOTTI BEANS In the UK we most often see borlotti beans in cans or dried, so when we grow them, we want to dry them. Drying is one of the oldest forms of preserving and can be one of the least practical. When making a minestrone soup, you want to add some of your borlotti, then you remember they're dried and you have to soak them overnight . . .

So just shell them when the pods are starting to shrivel up (that's when the bean is at its optimum), then freeze them without blanching. This way, you can use them straight away and they'll cook from frozen in 40 minutes and from fresh in 30. You'll be using them in winter dishes anyway – stews, casseroles, minestrone, soups, risotto – which take longer to cook. There are many varieties of borlotti and often you'll find the same one is a climber and a dwarf.

Lamon: Possibly the most famous of all the borlotti beans. Like many of the best beans in Italy, it comes originally from the Veneto region and is used to make only one dish: Pasta e Fagioli. To make it, you can use any borlotti bean, but to re-create it properly, you must use Lamon. It is the Rolls Royce of borlotti beans and has the characteristics needed to make the dish perfect.

Vigevano: From Liguria – there are two borlotti varieties from this area, a dwarf and a climber, and both are of excellent quality. You should sow in succession to have a continuous harvest in about 70 days. Each pod will contain about seven beans.

Lingua di Fuoco: A good all-round borlotti bean, again available in both climbing and dwarf. This variety, while being average, is very reliable and each pod will contain about seven beans.

Saluggia: This comes from the alpine region of Piedmont, not far from my family's home, and is an excellent variety. It is used locally to make the most wonderful risottos.

Centofiamme: A climbing variety, which is used nationally all over Italy. The name, 'hundred flames', reflects its coloration, as it is bright red on white. A good all-round variety.

Sanguino: Literally 'bloody', the name is due to its coloration. A very good national variety.

Stregonta: A climbing variety that is ready 70–75 days after sowing and that is excellent both for soups and stews.

Albenghino: A green borlotti bean from Liguria. This variety is a climber and the seeds are 'caffe-latte' coloured. Each 12–13 cm pod will contain six or seven meaty beans. Very productive.

CANNELLINI BEANS Unlike borlotti beans, cannelloni beans don't freeze well so are recommended for eating fresh and drying. There are several varieties but very little difference between them, so any one is fine to grow, planting when the ground is starting to warm up from April or May onwards.

CHICKPEAS At the RHS show at Hampton Court a few years back we had a little show garden (which won a Bronze) in which we had a container full of chickpeas. Everyone who came past said that it was impossible to grow them in the UK, yet there they were. What else can I do to convince people?

Although we associate chickpeas with Greece, Florence is one of the centres for these wonderful beans. The plants are dwarf and produce many pods, each containing two to three chickpeas. They can be eaten fresh, dried for later or frozen for no more than two months.

LENTILS Lentils are annual plants, so you have to sow them every year, starting from April or May until July. Obviously the later you sow, the later you'll harvest and a July sowing will give you a harvest around October. Sow the seed in fine soil, 4–5 cm deep. The plant is small and bushy, reaching a height of about 40–50 cm, so just treat it like a dwarf bean.

Lenticchie: Mid/early variety. A small green/grey Italian lentil. It has small, intense green leaves and produces numerous pods in which the lentils can be found. Sow from March to July.

BROAD BEANS You can sow broad beans in the autumn from September to November and again in the spring from February to April, as they like a bit of cold and will happily grow outside until the large green pods have swelled and they are ready to be harvested. They will germinate at 4°C, flower at 12°C and mature at 16°C, so you can see the growing cycle and when you can expect to harvest them. They will tolerate as low as -4°C, but any colder and they will croak.

Blanch broad beans before freezing to obtain best results. If you dry them, soak them at least overnight before using. You can also use them fresh. One of the best Sicilian varieties, which gives high-quality green broad beans, is not widely available as seed production is local.

Superaguadulce: The name means 'super sweet water' and refers to the juiciness and sweetness of this variety, which is probably the best of all – restaurant quality. Mid/early, the plant is vigorous and can grow to about a metre or slightly over. The pods are about 25–28 cm in length and each one will contain six to eight light green broad beans of good size and flavour.

Aguadulce Supersimonia: A mid/early garden variety, producing green pods about 30 cm long. Each pod contains eight to nine broad beans and the plant will reach about 120 cm in height.

Lunga delle Cascine: This literally translates as 'long of the farmhouse'. It's a popular variety with the restaurant trade and restaurant growers as it produces smaller broad beans that are very tender. It is a bit earlier than many other varieties. Each pod contains six to seven beans.

My Aunty Rose and Uncle Battista on their wedding day, pictured outside the famous Bianchi's in the Italian Quarter, Soho. My Nonna and Uncle Divo are also in this lovely, historical London picture of Italian life.

French Beans These are beans where you eat the whole pod rather than shelling them. French beans have a lot of benefits: they are easy to cook, useful in a multitude of dishes, meaty and tasty, and one of the most complete and nutritionally beneficial vegetables. They can help fight everything from cardiovascular diseases, obesity, anaemia and constipation to cancers and insomnia, and should be fed especially to children and convalescents.

Insalata di Cornetti
CORNETTI BEAN SALAD

In the summer, this dish is quick to make, healthy and delicious. The beans are stringless and tasty, like eating butter. SERVES 4

500 g cornetti beans (Meraviglia di Venezia) or French beans (Brittle Beurre), trimmed
extra-virgin olive oil
balsamic vinegar (preferably from Modena)
salt and freshly ground black pepper

BOIL THE BEANS IN A LARGE PAN OF WATER for about 8 minutes or until tender. Remove, place in a colander and cool under a cold tap. Place in a tea towel to remove any excess water, then add to a large bowl and season to taste with oil, vinegar, salt and pepper.

Fagiolini della Nonna Elena

NONNA ELENA'S FRENCH BEANS

I remember when I was courting my now wife in London I would often get home from work and Mum would have prepared a meal big enough to feed a football team. I would eat then go to see Alessandra, where upon arrival I would be greeted with another meal big enough to feed a football team. And I had to eat it and enjoy, or risk offending the family of the woman I loved . . . Italian etiquette can get very complicated, even in London!

My wife had been nagging me to include her mum's recipe for French beans, so when she gave it to me, I expected it to be called Mamma Silvia's Fagiolini. I had not realized that this is yet another example of a handed-down recipe – from my mother-in-law's mother, Elena, from the Veneto region of Italy. This kind of dish can be cooked the day before and reheated, when it will have even more flavour. SERVES 4

olive oil for frying
1 onion, chopped
2 carrots, chopped
4–5 celery sticks, chopped
500 g green French beans, trimmed
1 tomato, diced

vegetable stock, made from a cube dissolved in
1 glass water
dried herbs
parsley, roughly chopped
salt and freshly ground black pepper

HEAT SOME OLIVE OIL in a deep frying pan and gently fry the onion, carrots and celery for 15 minutes until softened. Place the beans in the pan with the tomato and add the stock and a pinch of your favourite dried herbs.

Continue to gently simmer for 35–40 minutes, adding the parsley towards the end of cooking. What you are after is not bean soup, but a juicy dish with some cooking liquor into which you just can't help dipping your bread. Check the seasoning before serving.

French bean growing tips

French beans are easy to grow. Like people (which is how I see vegetables), they come in many shapes, sizes, colours and flavours. There are green, yellow, purple and speckly ones, wide ones, stringless, long, short, early, late, heavy croppers, purple flowers, white flowers, etc. The fact that they are different is good because it gives you different cropping dates. Although they freeze well, you don't want too much of a glut. Go for an early bean like Ferrari, then one that crops all summer, like Koala, then a late variety, like the beautiful Meraviglia di Venezia.

Climbing beans need support in the form of canes or wire, but an existing wire fence will do, or the beans will safely grow up raspberry canes. Plant one seed 2–3 cm deep every 3–4 cm after the soil has warmed up – from April onwards – in rows 30 cm apart.

GREEN The most commonly used of all the French beans, even these vary greatly and come in all shapes and sizes. There are so many varieties, I will just give a brief outline.

Boby Bianco: Restaurateurs can buy Italian boby beans at New Covent Garden market. They are restaurant-quality, stringless, meaty dwarf beans. A white-seeded variety with beans typically reaching 12 cm in length.

La Victoire: French variety, a very fine, thin and elegant stringless dwarf bean. It has a black seed and will produce pods that are about 15 cm in length.

Vanguard: Franchi 'look after' this variety and are the original suppliers of the seeds listed in other catalogues. A good, reliable, stringless dwarf bean. Vanguard beans are typically about 15 cm in length and are ideal for the freezer.

S. Anna: Productive climbing pencil pod (round pod), which should be harvested from July to the end of September. The beans will reach about 14 cm in length.

Marconi: Green Roma bush-type bean, ready about 55 days after sowing. Good production on an upright plant. It is very crisp and tasty when picked small. Sow in succession every three weeks for a continuous harvest.

Supermarconi and Smeraldo: This is the Roma-type bean found in markets all over Italy. Begin picking when they are 12–15 cm long, but they will still be tender at 25 cm. They make wonderful bean salad. This vigorous climber needs support: use trellis, tripods or single poles at least 2.2 m tall. Plant after the soil has warmed up, since the seeds are not treated. Place three or four seeds around the base of each pole or, in the case of trellis, two seeds every 10 cm. Thin to one plant every 15 cm for trellis and two plants per pole. Like all climbing beans, keep picking to encourage continued production. You can harvest about 65 days after sowing.

Bobis a Grano Nero: Black-seeded, stringless, climbing, pencil pod, which can reach 180–190 cm in height. The pods are 12–13 cm in length and the plant is reliably productive.

Koala: A professional dwarf variety that harvests in bunches in succession over a long period through the whole summer. Stringless and very productive.

Anellino di Trento: Aka Anellino Marmorizzato. This is a very attractive northern Italian speciality. It is a curved dwarf bean, green with red/brown mottling, and has the flavour of a Roma bean.

Anellino di Brescia: An early variety with a mottled cream-coloured seed with red stripes. The curved, stringless pods look like large green shrimps. They are 10–11 cm long and very meaty.

Signora della Campagna: Worth growing just to see the beautiful pods. Vigorous with an excellent taste. The pods can be eaten whole when young or picked after about 75 days for shelling. Keep picking to encourage continued production. Grow on a tripod, single poles or mesh. For poles, sow four or five beans around the base, thinning to two or three plants; for trellis, sow two beans every 15 cm and thin to one.

Ferrari: As its name suggests, Ferrari is an early bean that grows very quickly. All the beans mature at once and are the same length within about a week. This makes it good for freezing. Beans are stringless and should be sown in succession if you want more than one harvest.

YELLOW

Meraviglia di Venezia: These Venetian wide, flat beans are the king of the yellow beans and give the green ones a run for their money too. They are meaty but tender and just melt in the mouth. They make the best bean salad, boiled then dressed with a vinaigrette while still warm. There are both climbing and dwarf examples and they will reach about 20 cm in length.

Meraviglia di Piemonte: Similar to the Meraviglia di Venezia, these beans from Piedmont are mottled like borlotti beans, but turn yellow when cooked. They are wide, stringless and meaty.

Brittle Buerre or Brittle Wax: This fine stringless yellow bean has a round pencil pod and can reach 14 cm in length. Harvest mid June to mid October.

Neckargold: A long, round, yellow climber of Dutch origin, with excellent taste. These are slim and crisp and ready in about 65 days.

PURPLE Purple beans turn green when you cook them, which is a shame as their colour is so attractive. Steaming preserves a little of their colour.

Purple King: A dwarf variety of which there is also a Purple Queen. Stringless, it produces numerous purple pods about 12 cm long.

Trionfo Violetto: This is an Italian variety whose name translates to 'purple triumph'. It is a climber and should be supported. Slightly curved, stringless, meaty and about 15 cm long, it also has a very good flavour.

Peas One of my earliest memories is of shelling peas with my mother. I can picture a balmy sunny day with all the windows open and a big bowl of green pods in the middle of the table – one of life's little pleasures.

Peas are an international species; you find them in every country and in many dishes from Europe to Asia. They are versatile, too, in that you can eat them fresh or store them for a week or so in the refrigerator. Frozen, bottled or canned, they keep their characteristics well.

Mangetout, sugar snap and snow peas are eat-all varieties. The flat, crunchy pods are eaten raw, boiled or used in stir-fries. They can be fully cooked until soft, but they are best half cooked, so they still have some crunch. The string is removed before eating.

RISI BISI by Andy Needham, Zafferano

This dish from Venice is basically a risotto with peas. I've given precise quantities but when I make risotto I find that 2 handfuls of rice per person gives an adequate portion. SERVES 4

80 g pancetta or bacon, cubed
30 g butter, plus a knob of butter for glazing
1 tablespoon olive oil
1 small onion, roughly chopped
350 g fresh peas (frozen or canned can be used if fresh are not available)

1 litre chicken stock
300 g risotto rice
chopped parsley
80 g Parmesan cheese, grated
salt and freshly ground black pepper

FRY THE PANCETTA OR BACON in the butter and oil. (A combination of butter and oil fries very efficiently.) After about a minute add the onion to the pancetta and fry for a further 2 minutes but don't let the onion brown. Add the peas and moisten with a cupful of the stock. Cook this gently for a further 6 minutes and then add the rice. All you want to do here is warm the rice through for a minute, stirring it so that it gets coated with some of the oil and flavours from the pancetta, then add the rest of the stock.

Turn the heat right down and simmer very gently, stirring occasionally, until the rice is cooked (usually about 20 minutes, though it can be quicker depending on the rice). Good risotto rice will remain slightly al dente anyway. Add a little more liquid (water or stock) towards the end if it starts to dry up and stick. When all the stock has been absorbed, taste for seasoning and then stir in a knob of butter, some parsley to taste and the Parmesan to lift the flavour and texture and add richness. Always serve risotto with wine, never with water: it is said that rice grows in water and dies in wine.

Carciofi Marinati con Burrata e Piselli

MARINATED ARTICHOKES WITH BURRATA AND PEAS

by Andy Needham, Zafferano

Condimento morbido is a white, sweet and sour vinegar, obtained by mixing fresh vinegar with Trebbiano grape must and then ageing the blend in barriques. It belongs to the same family as balsamic vinegar, but is better adapted to dressings and marinades.

Burrata is a fresh cheese from Puglia, made by blending mozzarella with cream and enclosing the mixture in a 'sack' made from pasta filata, the basis of mozzarella. SERVES 8

6 shallots, diced

100 ml red wine vinegar

3 green tomatoes, quartered and deseeded

2 tablespoons basil oil

3 tablespoons condimento morbido

60 g pea shoots

about 60 ml Tuscan or similar peppery olive oil

120 g fresh peas, cooked

300 g burrata

about 48 pieces marinated artichokes, halved

chives

salt

MARINATE THE SHALLOTS in the wine vinegar for 3 hours or more.

Blend the tomatoes in a food processor. Transfer to a chinois and squeeze out any excess juice. Combine the tomato purée with the basil oil, salt and a little condimento morbido.

Form into eight teaspoon-sized quenelles. Dress the pea shoots with a little Tuscan oil and condimento morbido. For each portion, pile the pea shoots over a bed of peas. To one side, spoon the burrata and put a green tomato quenelle on top. Pat the marinated artichokes dry and coat them lightly with oil and condimento morbido. Arrange six pieces between the burrata and the pea shoots. Sprinkle some shallots and chives on top. Sommelier's suggested accompaniment: Cayega (Tenuta Carretta) – a dry, pale yellow Piedmontese wine made from Arneis grapes, which has a floral, fruity nose with a mineral aftertaste.

Pea growing tips

The great thing about peas is that they are easy to grow and they like the cold, so you can sow them twice a year, in the spring and autumn, 2 cm apart. They are nitrogen-fixers and, growing with cold in the winter, don't deplete the soil of nutrients needed by other plants in the spring. It's great to sow them in October and then go indoors and forget all about them. Come the first nice spring day, you'll see pea plants spreading all over the ground almost ready for podding. Despite this winter hardiness, most people tend to only plant them once a year, in the spring.

Some peas climb but most are dwarf or half height and so may need support, and would certainly benefit in exposed, windy gardens. Although they have tendrils that grip on when climbing you still need to tie them with twine to help them along. The flowers are beautiful, especially in winter. They are white and purple and similar to the sweet pea.

There is some confusion between the names mangetout, snow pea and sugar snap. In Britain we use the term 'mangetout' to describe the family as a whole, while a snow pea is a flat-podded variety and a sugar snap pea is more swollen. Like all peas, they should be sown between September and November and February and April, 2 cm deep.

Rondo: A nice pea, mid/early, which grows about 70 cm tall with six to eight peas in each pod. It is a variety most suited to freezing.

Telefono: Late. Telefono is quite old-fashioned in that it is a climbing variety. This means that harvesting is easier and slugs can't get at it. The pods are straight, about 10–11 cm in length, and each pod does well, containing eight to ten peas. Telefono is a permanent fixture in my garden.

Piccolo Provenzale: Early. It is a smooth-skinned pea and the plant is only 40 cm tall. The intense green pod is straight and about 7–9 cm long, containing seven or eight peas. This is my favourite dwarf pea, really fresh and a lovely garden variety.

San Cristoforo: Saint Christopher is a climbing pea that reaches 140–150 cm in height. The pods are a light green colour and contain eight to nine peas. The peas are picked on the feast of Saint Christopher, 25 July.

Meraviglia d'Italia: 'Marvel of Italy' is a dwarf pea variety at 45 cm tall. Each pod is 9–10 cm long and contains seven to nine peas. This is a national variety and is grown in all regions.

Carouby Taccola Gigante: A late mangetout variety from Switzerland. The plant is 160 cm tall, so will need staking, and the straight green pods are 10–11 cm long. A good stir-fry variety and for general use in the kitchen.

Kelvedon Wonder: Early variety from near Colchester in Essex that is also grown in Italy, such is its quality. The pods are short at 8–9 cm and contain seven to eight peas.

Sweetcorn Corn, or maize, was one of the great discoveries from the Americas brought back by explorers such as Columbus and those who followed. It is a staple in many countries from Europe to Africa. In Zimbabwe they put left-over cornmeal in water to ferment, making a mild 'beer' called maheu that even the children drink.

In Italy, dried and ground corn is used to make polenta. It is cooked with water (and/or milk) and some salt into a stiff porridge and is pure peasant food. The northern Italians ate so much polenta in hard times, when it was the only food source available, that the southern Italians call them polentoni (polenta eaters).

Like all staples – bread, rice, pasta, etc. – polenta is quite bland. But, when you start adding Italian sausages in a rich tomato sauce with porcini mushrooms, layers of Fontina cheese and ham, baccalà (salt cod) Parma style with tomatoes and onions, game or Toma and Fontina cheeses and blackened alpine butter as in mountain-style Polenta Cunscia, then that's when you appreciate the polenta. Its blandness allows you to enjoy the flavours of the pietanze. Pietanze means and implies 'poor accompaniments' and would have been anything you could find to enrich the dish from milk and cheese to herbs, meats or vegetables.

To make your own polenta flour, dry the cobs, rub them together to remove the kernels and then grind to a coarse powder. I use a coffee grinder (cleaned out) on a coarse setting and this works well for me. This raw flour takes at least 30–45 minutes to cook, stirring very often, in salted boiling water. You can buy pre-cooked 5-minute polenta from your local Italian deli or supermarket, although the flavour will not be the same. Tradition calls for a copper pot and a wooden spoon: while a normal pot will be fine, stick to the wooden spoon for the stirring.

The funny thing is that Italians, especially the older generation, view sweetcorn itself (as in corn on the cob) as animal food. I remember once when I was young and on holiday in our village, where corn grows everywhere, I nicked a whole load of cobs with the idea of barbecuing them. The other kids looked at me as if I was mad – I might as well have nicked dog food! Times have changed and you can now find sweetcorn in cans in the shops, but that is about it.

Polenta Cunscia di Oropa
MOUNTAIN POLENTA FROM OROPA

The Santuario di Oropa is one of the most beautiful and special places for me. Situated in the mountains over Biella (Piedmont), where my family comes from, it's famous for its apparition of the black Madonna (black so she can be seen better against the snow) on a rock. It gets cold here, even in August. So the local dishes are hearty, rich, warming peasant dishes. SERVES 4

1 tablespoon salt
1 litre water
1 litre milk
250 g unsalted butter, plus extra for the polenta
350 g 'instant' polenta

a few sage leaves
1 kg Toma cheese, cut into small pieces
1 kg Fontina cheese, cut into small pieces
freshly ground black pepper

ADD THE SALT TO THE WATER AND MILK and bring to the boil with a knob of butter. Add the polenta flour bit by bit, stirring constantly at first to prevent lumpiness. Turn the heat down and simmer according to the packet instructions, stirring occasionally. Add more water if it looks too thick and dry. Put the butter into a pan with some sage leaves and gently fry until the butter is browned, but not burnt. Before serving, throw the cheese into the polenta, ensuring it melts in before serving in hot bowls. Pour a good shot of the melted nutty butter on top of each portion and add freshly ground black pepper. The black burnt butter specks are the key flavour.

Sweetcorn growing tips

Sow from April onwards until about June. Some people start it in pots then plant out; others just sow direct. Plant 2 cm deep and thin out to 10 cm. The plants reach about 150–180 cm in height, depending on the variety, and a good cob of corn should be about 20 cm or more in length. Aim for seven or eight plants every square metre.

Eating Sweetcorn: One of the best varieties is Zuccherino, which means 'sugary'. Sow April to June and harvest until the first frosts.

Polenta Mais: A good yellow variety for polenta is called Sisred. Leave the corn to dry on the plant. When harvesting, remove the outer leaves and make sure they dry out before milling.

Popcorn: This is a poor-quality corn not good enough for eating as sweetcorn, but ideal for popping. The corn is dried and then heated with a spoonful of oil in a lidded pan.

patate

POTATOES

The potato was a staple in the Americas and although Columbus didn't bring back much 'treasure' in the way of gold and silver, he did bring back corn and potatoes – a different kind of gold. It's probably the most cooked ingredient on the planet, even if you only count chips (or French fries if you're reading this in America!). Then we have crisps (or potato chips), mashed potato, gnocchi, baked potatoes, boiled potatoes, new potatoes... See what I mean!

Potatoes are about three-quarters water – like humans (bet this is the first time you've ever read a comparison between a person and a potato!) – and they are rich in mineral salts and vitamins, many of which are contained in the skin. They also contain sugars, so diabetics shouldn't go mad on them.

The best way to enjoy newly picked spuds is simply by just boiling them and serving with butter – honestly. They will amaze you with their sweetness and flavour and will win you over to their simple charm. It is because they are not sophisticated that they go so well with complex flavours like truffle and asparagus and work as a topping to, for example, fish pies.

GNOCCHI DI PATATE from Country House Montali

SERVES 4

For the dough

4 potatoes, yellow or red

¼ tablespoon butter

a pinch of salt

a pinch of nutmeg

2 egg yolks

70 g Italian '00' flour

70 g Grano Duro flour, plus more for dusting

1 handful of grapes

icing sugar for sprinkling

½ handful of chopped walnuts

For the cheese sauce

85 g Taleggio

45 g Emmental

45 g Provolone

45 g Pecorino di Pienza

150 ml milk

2 tablespoons single cream

1 tablespoon butter

COOK AND PEEL THE POTATOES. Push through a potato ricer on to a lightly floured surface and add the butter and salt. Work well with a spatula until evenly incorporated. Cover and cool completely. Add the nutmeg and egg yolks and work them into the potato with your hands until the dough is even in colour and texture. In batches, incorporate the two flours into the dough with the help of a pastry cutter. When the dough begins to come together, knead quickly and gently until even, adding more Grano Duro if too sticky.

Using a pastry cutter or knife, portion off 2 tablespoons of dough. Roll out on a lightly floured surface into a long 1-cm thick rope. Cut into 1 cm pieces. Gently press your index and middle fingers into the centre of one piece and slowly roll your fingers back towards you, allowing the dough to follow and form a shell shape. Repeat with the remaining dough, gently tossing batches with Grano Duro flour to avoid sticking. Set aside on a floured tray, making sure the pieces do not touch.

Grate all the cheeses and combine with the remaining sauce ingredients over a double boiler. Melt over simmering water, gently mixing continuously with a wooden spoon. When the sauce is creamy, remove from the heat and keep covered until serving.

Peel and halve the grapes. Gently remove the seeds and lay the halves face-down over a sheet of parchment paper. Barely sprinkle with icing sugar and bake at Gas Mark 4/180°C for 10 minutes. Transfer the cheese sauce to a sauté pan and heat gently.

Bring a pot of lightly salted water to a simmer and slide the gnocchi from the tray. As soon as the pieces come to the surface (approximately 1 minute), remove with a slotted spoon and place immediately into the sauce. Toss together and transfer to a large serving platter or individual plates. Garnish with chopped walnuts and baked grape halves and serve immediately.

GATEAU DI PATATE from Country House Montali

If smoked Provolone is not available use a different mild smoked cheese. SERVES 6

3 large potatoes
40 g butter
2 eggs, lightly beaten
2 tablespoons extra-virgin olive oil
2 tablespoons grated Parmesan cheese

1 tablespoon grated Pecorino cheese
olive oil for greasing
breadcrumbs
28 g smoked Provolone cheese, cut into small cubes
salt, black pepper and white pepper to taste

COOK AND PEEL THE POTATOES. Mash well with the butter in a bowl and cool. When at room temperature, mix in the remaining ingredients minus the oil for greasing, smoked cheese and breadcrumbs. Grease six 5 cm ramekins and dust with breadcrumbs. Layer the bottoms with a small piece of parchment paper.

Divide half the mixture among the ramekins. Layer with the smoked cheese cubes and top with the remaining mixture. Use the teeth of a fork to draw concentric circles over the top. Top with dots of butter, bake at Gas Mark4/180°C.

'Tutto fumo e niente arrosto'

ALL SMOKE AND NO ROAST

Potato growing tips

I always said that I would never grow potatoes because they can be bought so cheaply in the shops. Surely it would be more sense to grow asparagus, which costs £2.99 a bunch? And so I did. Then, one day, I sampled a home-grown, just-pulled spud from someone's plot and it blew my mind. The flavour was amazing – sweet and intense – and the texture was fluffy and buttery. So now I grow potatoes and they can rival my tomatoes any day.

Potatoes are easy to grow in that you don't have to sow seeds, like with a tomato, but seed potatoes, which often look like shrivelled-up old spuds from the back of the fridge but in reality are clean (disease-free), thoroughbred varieties that will grow true and give a good crop. Don't be tempted to plant your old potatoes that have sprouted under the stairs as the outcome will be variable and you can't be sure about disease, especially the dreaded potato blight, which also affects tomatoes.

They will germinate between 16 and 29 days at 12°C, flower 36 to 40 days later, and mature after another 50 to 60 days, giving a total 'days to maturity' of 102–129, depending on the variety. You can force them by planting them in heated beds from December and, generally speaking, you can continue to plant potatoes up until the end of spring. Plant 5–7 cm deep, leaving 25–30 cm between each seed potato. Make sure that you water in dry periods.

The flowers, the sprouting shoots and green bits on a potato contain toxins. This is why you should keep potatoes in the dark as it is the light that increases the toxins and turns the potato green. It probably won't kill you, but it may upset your stomach or make you feel nauseous, so throw any dodgy potatoes away and remove any shoots.

You should harvest them before the leaves start to die back. If you're not sure, dig down a little to see what you've got. Potatoes can spread out, so do dig about 30–40 cm around the plant. When you have harvested them, leave them to dry outside for at least a day in the sun or in a warm airy place as they will store better. Be sure to dispose of the plants by composting them well. If you have had the blight (you can still eat the potatoes) then please burn the plants and disinfect your fork and tools.

There are literally thousands of varieties: yellow-fleshed, white-fleshed and even purple. In Italy the main areas of production are Liguria, the Veneto region, Piedmont, Emilia, the Marche and Naples, and in Sicily in Catania, Messina and Palermo. Here are two of my favourites.

Spunta: A yellow-fleshed variety from Messina in Sicily, which is a second early/main crop and prized for its flavour. A very good potato for salads and for frying.

Primura: One of the most popular varieties in Italy and typical of the Bologna area. It is oval in shape with white/pale yellow flesh of high quality, early and productive. A good all-round potato.

altre *verdure*

OTHER VEGETABLES

Other vegetables refers to anything that is not covered in any of the other sections but is a mainstay of the back garden – spinach, beetroot, kale, cabbage, carrots and everything else you couldn't live without!

In a similar way as this book, it is a good idea to have your veg plot laid out as you might ingredients in your kitchen. Try the following as a guide to five areas: herbs (in pots or in the ground); leaves for salad (from lettuces, chicories, lambs lettuce, radicchio, rocket and the like); a cloche, poly-tunnel or greenhouse with Mediterranean veg (peppers, aubergine, cucumbers, etc); other veg outside (this should be the largest plot and when you harvest something you should sow something) and a miscellaneous area with strawberries (in pots is fine), potatoes in potato bags, mushroom logs, fruit bushes, rhubarb, additional salad leaves growing in grow bags – things like that.

Nothing is fixed in stone and you can plant things where you have spaces. If you have a failure, and even the most experienced person can't beat nature sometimes, then accept it and just sow something else. Keep it fluid, keep sowing. It's not rocket science and you will learn as you go. Just sow and see what happens.

Agretti This is difficult to describe, like describing a truffle. It has some other names: barba di frate (monk's beard), roscano and salsola soda. It's a mild-flavoured green, which is a little bit bitter, but a lot wonderful. Really only known in Rome (Lazio generally) and Umbria, it's impossible to find in the UK and very, very gastronomic. It's a bit like sea samphire, but you grow it in the ground rather than on salt marshes, which, let's face it, not many of us have in our back gardens.

It's the flavour that makes agretti so alluring. It tastes like spinach, asparagus and sea water, and looks like chives with fat, rounded leaves. Agretti goes well with fish and seafood. You can use it raw in salads or you can cook it and use it in pasta. Try it braised with a little garlic and served as a side dish, boiled and served with olive oil, or take a large handful and slap a sea bass in the middle to steam.

Agretti growing tips

Agretti grows very easily, tolerating cold, heat, wet or dry, but it is an absolute bastard to get viable seeds from – and that isn't too strong a word! That's why you probably don't know what it is: it's so volatile and unpredictable that some years we have it and other years we don't. The seed will keep for only a few months, hence its rarity. Most seed companies won't touch it with a barge pole, but if you can get hold of it then try and grow some, because it is a worthwhile ingredient.

Sow – when you have viable seed – any time from February to November. Cover seeds with 1 cm of soil and space 10 cm apart. Thin to one plant every 16–20 cm apart in a row or raised bed. Germination takes between seven and ten days. When mature (in about 50 days) they form a bush 30 cm wide, 60 cm high. You can start cutting from the plants when they are about 20 cm tall. Cut the green tops or sections of the plant; it will then regrow.

This picture of my grandparents could well be anywhere in Italy, but is in fact in the family home, where my mum was born (during an air raid) in Brentmead Place, Hendon.

Artichokes The globe artichoke is in fact the unopened flower of a plant that was bred from the cardoon, so the two are related. They were at first grown in Naples and Rome, due to the favourable conditions, where they were often eaten with Mentuccia, a type of mint.

Artichokes are rich in vitamin C, potassium and iron, so they are great for people, like me, with Crohn's disease, who need all three of these elements.

To eat them, you boil them until a skewer goes through them easily – depending on their size this can take about 30 minutes. Take each leaf off and dip the fleshy part into a good vinaigrette; eat this meaty part, leaving just the hard outer leaf. As you get further into the artichoke, the leaves become more and more tender. Then you get to the prize in the middle which is the cuore, the heart at the base of the fruit where the stalk begins, and this is better than chocolate any day. Sweet, juicy and meaty with a delicate flavour. You must remove the fibres (the choke) that surround the heart because they are 'poisonous' at certain times of the year. I'm not sure if this is actually true or whether it's just one of those things your parents tell you when you are little, like that mortadella is made from donkeys!

Carciofi alla Romana
ARTICHOKES ROMAN STYLE

I was lucky enough to work for British Airways for eight years and during that time I went to Rome with Alex while we were still courting. We were both skint and just went for one night. Because we had got a great deal on the hotel we were able to splash out on dinner at a restaurant near the Fontana di Trevi. What we ordered was artichokes. It would be a bit like going to Cornwall and not eating a pasty or to Somerset and not drinking cider. It is a meal that we have always remembered. Here is a little taste of Rome. SERVES 4

8 cooked artichokes (with stalk if possible)
juice of 1 lemon
3 tablespoons parsley
1 tablespoon mint

2 cloves of garlic
½ wine glass olive oil
salt and freshly ground black pepper

REMOVE THE TOUGHER OUTER LEAVES of the artichokes until you have left only the tenderest parts, and leave about 5 cm of stalk. Immerse each artichoke in water to clean, and then place in a bowl with cold water and some lemon juice (or wine vinegar), so as to keep their colour.

Chop the parsley, mint and garlic, add to the olive oil and season to taste. Open up the artichokes and stuff with some of this mixture, then place in a saucepan, with the stalks pointing upwards. Pour the rest of the mixture around the artichokes so that the hearts are just covered, then add water with a little lemon juice up to the level of the stalks.

Simmer gently until the water has evaporated, and serve hot.

Tagliolini con Carciofi e Prosciutto
TAGLIOLINI WITH ARTICHOKES AND PARMA HAM
by Franco Taruschio

Use the Viola or Violetti variety of globe artichokes for this dish. They are small and have no hairy chokes (or very little), so once the outer leaves are removed the whole artichoke can be eaten. Although we have suggested using Parma ham here, in the Marche prosciutto di Carpegna or prosciutto nostrano would be used. These are available from good Italian delicatessens. The artichoke sauce can be prepared in advance and then reheated for serving. SERVES 4

juice of 1 lemon
4 artichokes
4 tablespoons extra-virgin olive oil
50 g Parma ham, cut in julienne strips
2 large spring onions, trimmed and chopped
6 tablespoons dry white wine

6 tablespoons water
400 g fresh tagliolini
salt and freshly ground black pepper
chopped flat-leaf parsley and Parmesan cheese
  shaving, to garnish

PREHEAT THE OVEN to Gas Mark 6/200°C. Have ready a large bowl of cold water to which the lemon juice has been added.

Wash and trim the artichokes and remove the hard outer leaves. If the tops of the remaining leaves are hard, trim off approximately 2.5 cm. Cut each artichoke lengthways into six and put into the bowl of lemon water.

Heat the olive oil in a small flameproof casserole and fry the ham and spring onions for 1–2 minutes. Drain the artichokes, add them to the pan and cook over a moderate heat, stirring frequently, for 10 minutes.

Add the wine and allow to evaporate. Add the water, then cover the casserole and transfer to the oven. Cook for about 20 minutes or until the sauce is reduced and the artichokes are tender. Season with salt and pepper.

Meanwhile, bring a large saucepan of lightly salted water to the boil and cook the tagliolini until al dente. Drain and tip into a large, warmed serving bowl. Pour the sauce over the pasta, scatter over the parsley and Parmesan shavings and serve immediately.

Torta di Bistecca, Carciofi e Farro

BEEF, ARTICHOKE AND SPELT PIE

Beef and artichokes work well together, like beef and oysters, and make a rich, filling and flavoursome meal. It's an easy dish to make. The filling will simmer away slowly and cook itself (you just have to remember to stir it), then you cover with pastry and bake it in the oven. It can be prepared the day before and baked fresh on the day.

Farro (spelt) can be grown easily. It is simple to cook (just boil it), and it has a chewy texture and nutty flavour. It can also be bought canned and ready to use. SERVES 4

675 g braising steak
flour
olive oil
thyme, chopped
sage leaves, chopped
1 onion (Ramata di Milano), roughly chopped
2 cloves of garlic (Bianco Veneto), chopped
1 glass red wine

tomato purée
anchovy paste
2 large fresh artichoke hearts (Romanesco) or a
*   200 g jar artichoke hearts, diced*
140 g spelt, cooked (either boiled or ready canned)
500 g shortcrust pastry
salt and freshly ground black pepper

CUT THE STEAK INTO 2.5 CM CUBES and toss in a plate of seasoned flour.

Put some oil in a heavy pan with a lid and, when hot, add the meat to brown. Cover and stir occasionally. Season and add a good pinch of fresh chopped thyme and sage. When almost brown, add the onion and garlic and stir in, lowering the heat to medium and covering again.

After 3–5 minutes, pour in the wine and flavour with a little tomato purée and anchovy paste. Cover, and set a timer for 1½ hours. Stir every now and then. When the time is up. Add the artichoke hearts and spelt. There should be some good gravy, but you can always add more liquid if necessary.

Pour into an ovenproof dish and cover with a rolled-out piece of pastry to fit. Make a hole in the centre to allow air to escape and bake at Gas Mark 6/200°C for about 15 minutes until golden brown.

Serve with red wine and rustic bread.

Artichoke growing tips

You can sow artichokes both in the spring and in the autumn (August to September). Sow 2 cm deep in a tray and then transplant into the garden later when you have a nice plant and the weather has warmed. The general rule is to sow them this year for next, but if you sow early in the spring and plant out in early summer, you can get small artichokes the same year. At the end of the year, cut the plants back to 2 cm and cover with some straw, and they will come back to life again in the spring. The plants are large – 2 m tall with quite a big 'wing span' – so do consider whether you have enough space before you decide to grow them. That said, they are very architectural and add depth to a garden; the flowers are also beautiful and, if not eaten, can be kept and dried.

Some varieties have lethal spikes, so always wear gloves when picking these. The spiky ones are typical of Sicily, for example, but are found all over Italy. They are worth growing because they have a good flavour. The spineless ones, though, are more user-friendly and so a lot of these are produced.

There are purple artichokes and green ones and both are used in Italy, France and Spain, which are the main producers, although California produces most of the artichokes for the US according to our US Franchi seed distributor, Bill Mckay. Based in Boston, with an Irish father and an Italian mother, Bill has a tough exterior and is a straight talker, but I know him well and he is just like an artichoke – with a soft centre and the kindest heart – and he's a really good grower, which is how he got started. This is definitely the first time I have ever compared anyone to an artichoke!

Green Globe: Produces a large, green globe that has thick meaty sheaths but is quite strong in flavour and quite clumsy gastronomically. It suits dishes in which you might want a stronger artichoke flavour.

Violetto: There are different purple varieties from Rome (Romanesco) and two from Venice (Chioggia and Sant'Erasmo), but there are also others. Their characteristics are similar in that the globes are slightly smaller, generally speaking, than the green varieties but the flavour is much more delicate and gastronomically superior.

Cardoons The part of the plant that you eat is the stalk, which has something of the flavour of cooked celery. Cardoons are not eaten all that much in the UK, which is a shame because they are very low in calories and they have a nice flavour, not as strong as celery but with the subtleness of an artichoke.

Cardoons are not used widely in Italy either, but in Piedmont, where the most important variety comes from, they are used a lot both as a cooked vegetable and also raw with the famous dish Bagna Cauda, which is made with anchovies, garlic, parsley, butter, oil and, sometimes, cream.

Cardi Piemontesi

PIEDMONTESE CARDOONS

Cardoons are eaten widely across Piedmont. This is a gratin-style recipe from the same region that also works very well with fennel. Gratins are quite common in this area, influenced by proximity to France and the abundance of good mountain cheeses. SERVES 4

700 g Gobbo di Nizza cardoons
lemon juice
400 ml Béchamel sauce

butter
100 g freshly grated Parmesan cheese
salt

CLEAN THE CARDOONS IN WATER with added lemon juice, removing any filaments. Simmer in slightly salted water until cooked. This can take from 30 minutes up to an hour, depending on the size and type of cardoon, but when a skewer goes through them easily, you know they are done.

Drain the cardoons and transfer to an ovenproof dish. Pour the Béchamel sauce over them and place some specks of butter on top. Sprinkle with the grated Parmesan and cook at Gas Mark 6/200°C for about 20 minutes until the top has lightly browned.

BAGNA CAUDA

It is fascinating that anchovies have become so much a part of the food of Piedmont, although it does not border the sea. The reason for their popularity is that merchants would take their goods to the ports to be shipped and then, rather than come back empty handed, would load up with the salty little fish. Bagna Cauda means 'hot sauce' and it makes the best dip or dressing for crunchy vegetables like peppers, celery, cardoons, radicchio leaves or carrot sticks. SERVES 4

120 g anchovies (rinsed, if salted)
5 cloves of garlic, finely sliced
milk
cardoons (or other crunchy vegetables), for dipping
lemon juice

60 g unsalted butter
275 ml olive oil
a bunch of parsley, chopped
country-style rustic bread

FILLET THE ANCHOVIES IF NECESSARY, mash and place in a bowl. Marinate the garlic slices in a little milk for a couple of hours. Wash the cardoons, cut each piece to include some heart, and place in cold water with some lemon juice.

Gently heat the butter and oil in a saucepan and add the anchovy paste. Strain the garlic from the milk and add it to the oil, stirring occasionally. Continue to gently heat for 20 minutes. Remove from the heat and add the parsley. Using a fondue set or hotplate, place the Bagna Cauda mixture on a low heat. Each person should take a piece of cardoon and dip it into the mixture, eating it with the rustic bread and some red wine from Piedmont.

Cardoons growing tips

Cousins of the artichoke, cardoons are a winter vegetable, sown from March to June and harvested with the cold. You have to blanch the stalks, blocking out as much light as possible (I use tin foil), otherwise they will be bitter and tough. Cardoons are not easy vegetables to grow, but I have had some success with them and, because I like them and they're hard to find, I'll continue to grow them.

Gobbo di Nizza Monferrato: A vigorous plant that produces fruits with thick ribs that are almost spineless and curl around on themselves. It can be earthed up for blanching. Sow from March to the end of June.

Bianco Ivorio: Mid/late variety. A large, vigorous plant with crunchy, white, meaty ribs and serrated leaves without spines. Blanch before eating. Sow from March to June.

My Nonna Angela is on the right in this wonderful photo taken circa 1930
when she was a very young apprentice cook at the Hyde Park Hotel. All the chefs were from Piedmont
and it could be said that the London catering scene wouldn't run without Italian immigrants.
Ten years later, these young men would be in prison camps (like my grandfather) due to the Second World War.
The happiness shown in this picture only returned after the conflict ended.

Asparagus Asparagus is one of those seasonal products that you can't force or fool into producing at other times. You wait all year and then, all of a sudden, big fat spears of green or purple asparagus appear in the shops as if from nowhere.

Asparagus spears have a woody part and a tender part, which of course is the bit that you eat. An easy way to determine one from the other is simply to bend the spears, and they will naturally break at the point where the two meet, leaving you with the edible tender part. You can keep the woody parts to flavour the stock for making asparagus soup, but you must discard them or you'll have a chewy soup.

The other tip I would give is always to wash asparagus spears very well as they can be full of sand or grit. There's nothing worse than gritty chicken and asparagus pie.

Uova e Asparagi
EGG AND ASPARAGUS

This particular recipe comes from Emilia but there are similar recipes using these two ingredients from all over the world. Egg and asparagus go together like truffles and hounds... a marriage made in heaven, which tastes all the better because you can only eat it in asparagus season. Simple recipes are often the tastiest, and this is no exception. You need roughly 1 egg for every 50 g asparagus, once the woody part has been removed. The beauty of this dish is cutting into the egg yolk, which will run down on to the asparagus. Serve just with a doorstep of bread with butter. SERVES 4

500 g asparagus
8 eggs
butter

100 g Parmesan cheese, grated
salt

CLEAN AND WASH THE ASPARAGUS, removing the woody part from the fleshy part by bending the spears. They will snap where the two parts meet. Blanch the tender tips in slightly salted water for about 5–6 minutes until they are almost soft and then drain them.

Divide the spears between four terracotta ramekins (or place in one larger one) and carefully break 2 eggs into each ramekin, without breaking the yolks. Put some specks of butter on top of each egg and sprinkle with the Parmesan cheese.

Place in the oven at Gas Mark 5/190°C for 15 minutes or under a medium hot grill for about 10 minutes, until the egg whites are firm and the yolk are still soft.

Asparagi con Sugo di Bolzano

ASPARAGUS WITH BOLZANO SAUCE by Andrea Falter

On the Continent white asparagus is far more common and popular than in the UK. If you want to use white asparagus for this recipe, peel it completely and cook it for a good 20 minutes.

SERVES 4

1.2 kg green asparagus
60 g butter
1 teaspoon salt
a pinch of sugar
For the sauce
4 eggs
125 ml olive oil

1 teaspoon mustard
1 teaspoon lemon juice
2 tablespoons dry white wine
2 tablespoons chopped parsley
1 tablespoon chopped chives
salt and freshly ground black pepper

WASH THE ASPARAGUS and trim back the woody ends. Place the asparagus in a large pan and fill with water until just covered. Add the butter, salt and sugar and gently simmer for approximately 10 minutes.

Meanwhile, boil the eggs until hard, then rinse under cold water to make peeling easier. Separate the egg yolks, press through a sieve and mix slowly with the oil. Gradually add all the remaining ingredients and finish with folding in the chopped egg whites.

Arrange the asparagus on a warm plate and serve the sauce separately.

Asparagus growing tips

Originally called sparrow grass, asparagus forms crowns, or a root system (like rhubarb), and comes up in the spring. It is an ancient crop and has been around for centuries, originally as wild asparagus and then bred into the fatter varieties we know today. Some people say that asparagus takes three, five or even seven years to establish, but all the skill of growing it is in the preparation of the ground rather than in its maintainance, other than keeping the area weed-free.

To plant asparagus, you have to prepare a bed in advance by digging down to make the soil friable and adding some grit and manure at the bottom. To obtain very good asparagus it is advisable to prepare a long furrow. The transplant must be done correctly: the asparagus crowns should be positioned in a single row at the bottom of the furrow, 33 cm apart (about three per metre), making sure the roots lie horizontally. Cover them immediately with 5 cm of soil.

The general rule for harvesting is: first year, for every three spears that appear, pick one and leave two; second year, pick two and leave one; from the third year, pick all three. The only exception is wild asparagus, which can be picked the year after planting. It will never be fat and meaty. From the second year onwards, you can pick for weeks, sometimes until June. In summer put nitrogen fertilizer and water in the trench. In autumn the leaves will become yellow and dry, so cut them off. Keep the area clean of weeds. There are green, purple and white varieties and they all have different characteristics.

Green: Traditional green asparagus produces meaty spears, which can have a slight violet tinge to them. This is the type we are all very familiar with.

Purple: The variety most sought after in Italy is Violetto d'Albenga. It's a historic variety from Liguria, dating from at least 1570, when it was described in Bartolomeo Scappi's book *Dell'Arte del Cucinare*. It went into dangerous decline, not because of its quality, which is superior, but because to produce it commercially each plant has to be staked to grow on the terraces of Liguria and so it requires more work than regular varieties. It has been 'discovered' again recently and is highly prized for its superb quality and flavour. Mid/late harvest.

White: In the UK, we most often see white asparagus in tins. It is much more widely used in France and Spain, but in Italy it is used only in the Veneto region, where it is highly prized. The spears are very meaty, mid length and sweet but with a slight, pleasant, bitter aftertaste.

Wild – Scaber Montina: Excellent flavour makes this hard-to-find variety much sought after by chefs. It yields thin, tasty tips from small to medium crowns. Superior wild asparagus is precious, with high productivity, suitable for any climate and soil. Very good boiled or steamed and perfect for omelettes, risotto, pasta and with black truffles. Plant November to April.

Argenteuil: This French variety from the outskirts of Paris is available as seeds. They will take a year longer, as the first year the seeds make the crowns then the crowns start to make the asparagus. Growing asparagus from seed is cheaper than buying crowns, which cost at least £1.

Aubergines I used to be the only person in my household who liked aubergines (or eggplants, as they are known in most English-speaking countries), and I can understand why some do not like them. If you are one of those, then do try and make an Aubergine Parmigiana and see if you change your mind. This is exactly what happened with my wife, who always complained that aubergines just taste of the oil you fry them in.

They don't have a lot of flavour but they will bulk out dishes and have a unique texture. They are very low in fat and recent studies have shown that they may indeed even lower cholesterol. It is said that round aubergines are sweeter than long, and the other benefit of growing round ones is that you end up with nice round slices.

Before cooking aubergines it is advisable to place the slices on kitchen paper and sprinkle with salt to remove the excess (and bitter) water.

Melanzane alla Parmigiana
AUBERGINES PARMA STYLE

My father-in-law comes from this region and this is one of the dishes he likes to show off. It is very simple and even people who say they don't like aubergines are always surprised at how good it tastes. The number of layers doesn't matter too much as long as they are single (not overlapping or double layers) and that you end with tomato sauce and Parmesan on the top layer. SERVES 4

3 large aubergines
oil for frying
150 g fresh mozzarella, sliced
250 ml tomato-based pasta sauce

200 g Parmesan cheese, grated
fresh basil to taste
salt

WASH THE AUBERGINES, dry and then cut into 1 cm thick strips lengthways. Generously sprinkle with salt to draw out their bitter water, and place on a clean tea towel, turning after 30 minutes and repeating on the other side. Wash and dry to remove the excess salt.

Heat the oil in a frying pan. Fry the aubergines until lightly browned on both sides.

Arrange layers of aubergines, mozzarella, tomato sauce, then Parmesan and basil, in a baking dish, repeating to make a multi-layered dish. Bake at Gas Mark 4/180°C until warmed through and the Parmesan on top has lightly browned. Serve hot.

CAPONATA by Giorgio Locatelli

If you don't like fennel or celery, leave them out and increase all the other ingredients slightly. Keep in mind that this is not a fixed recipe; it is something that is done according to taste and you can change it as you like. SERVES 4

1 large aubergine

olive oil for frying

1 onion, cut into 2 cm dice

vegetable oil for deep-frying

2 celery sticks, cut into 2 cm dice

½ fennel bulb, cut into 2 cm dice

1 courgette, cut into 2 cm dice

3 fresh plum tomatoes, cut into 2 cm dice

a bunch of basil

50 g sultanas

50 g pine nuts

about 100 ml extra-virgin olive oil

5 tablespoons good-quality red wine vinegar

1 tablespoon tomato passata

1 tablespoon caster sugar

sea salt and freshly ground black pepper

CUT THE AUBERGINE INTO 2 CM CUBES, sprinkle with salt and leave to drain in a colander for at least 2 hours. Squeeze lightly to get rid of excess liquid.

Heat a little olive oil in a pan and gently sauté the onion until soft but not coloured. Transfer to a large bowl.

Put the vegetable oil in a deep-fat fryer or a large deep saucepan (no more than one third full) and heat to 180°C. Add the celery and deep-fry for 1–2 minutes, until tender and golden. Drain on kitchen paper.

Wait until the oil comes back up to the right temperature, then put in the fennel. Cook and drain in the same way, then repeat with the aubergine and courgette.

Add all the deep-fried vegetables to the bowl containing the onion, together with the diced tomatoes.

Tear the basil leaves and add them to the bowl with all the rest of the ingredients, seasoning well. Cover the bowl with cling film while the vegetables are still warm and leave to infuse for at least 2 hours before serving at room temperature. Don't put it in the fridge or you will dull the flavours. It is this process of 'steaming' inside the cling film and cooling down very slowly that changes caponata from a kind of fried vegetable salad, with lots of different tastes, to something with a more unified, distinctive flavour.

Aubergine growing tips

Aubergines are Mediterranean plants and so need to be sown protected in a greenhouse and then grown on protected in a greenhouse or polytunnel. Some years however (like 2006), when we have a good hot summer, they will grow on outside, but as this can be unreliable my advice is always to grow them indoors. This is in contrast to tomatoes, which are also Mediterranean in origin but have indoor and outdoor varieties for the UK.

I must say that it is worth getting a greenhouse if you don't have one already. I bought mine second-hand from a friend-of-a-friend for £80. It's a nice big one too, but Alex and I almost killed each other trying to assemble it without any instructions. We got there in the end though, and the benefit is that not only are we able to grow things like peppers, aubergines, indoor tomatoes, cucumbers and melons, but also that we can start crops earlier and finish picking later. In the winter I can cut fresh lettuce leaves, which I would not be able to do outside.

Aubergine seeds should be sown from February to May, 1 cm deep, in cells, small pots or trays and then planted into larger pots or in the ground in your greenhouse or polytunnel. You can also grow them in growbags, three per bag. Remember that the bags can dry out quickly, so be sure to water and to add tomato food too, as the plants can deplete the nutrients quickly.

There are some cultural differences between Britain and Italy: in Italy we tend to grow long aubergines or round white ones, while in Britain it tends to be mainly round black varieties.

Pianta delle Uova: Literally translated as 'egg plant'. It produces small white fruits that resemble eggs and range in colour from pale yellow to white. The leaves are intense green and of medium dimensions and this annual plant can also be grown ornamentally with much effect.

Black Beauty: Mid/early. Large round aubergine variety with black skin. The plant is vigorous and the fruits are medium sized.

Linda F1 (ex. Gitana): Early, productive plant with long, slightly curved, shiny black fruits. A very reliable variety, well suited to greenhouse cultivation. The fruits store well and are recommended for forcing.

Primato F1: Mid/early. A large, round/oval, shiny, black-skinned hybrid variety, which gives nice round slices. Suitable for outdoor cultivation if started early enough and planted in full sun.

Violetta Lunga: Mid/early. The classic Italian variety, with long, straight, black-skinned fruits.

Tondo Bianca Sfumato di Rosa: Mid/early. A white variety with a slight pink tinge, also known as Romanesco. The fruits are large with white flesh and few seeds and of excellent flavour.

Aubergine Prosperosa: Mid/early. The name of this round variety translates as 'prosperous', because it is a good variety for market. It has a shiny mauve skin and the fruits are medium sized with very few seeds inside.

Beetroot To cook beetroot, you should wash them and cut the stalks, leaving about 5 cm so that they don't bleed into the water. The first time I cooked them I didn't know to do this, and by the time the beetroots were cooked I had bright red water and almost white beetroot! You can eat beetroot hot, but I prefer them cold with cream cheese and a little olive oil and black pepper. In Poland I had a delicious cold Borscht soup, which was garnished with yogurt, cucumber slices and hard-boiled eggs.

BEETROOT CARPACCIO by Jim, Head Chef at The Granville

SERVES 4

4 large beetroot
olive oil
50 g pine nuts
150 g goat's cheese

snipped chives
juice of 1 lime
sea salt and freshly ground black pepper

WASH AND DRY THE BEETROOT. Place them on a roasting tray, drizzle with olive oil and shake to coat them. Cover with foil and roast in the oven for about an hour at Gas Mark 4/180°C until tender in the middle. When ready, place in the fridge to cool.

Toast the pine nuts under a grill. Leave them to cool then chop.

Before serving, remove the skin from the beetroot and slice thinly, using a mandoline or a very sharp knife. Lay the slices on a plate in a single layer. Crumble over the goat's cheese, then sprinkle with the pine nuts and chives. Pour over the lime juice and some olive oil, and serve.

Beetroot growing tips

Egitto: 'Egyptian'. Early. A semi-flat beetroot of medium dimensions with purple-red flesh. Sow from March to the end of July.

Tondo di Chioggia: From the Venice region. Early. A round red root with characteristic alternating white and red stripes inside. Sow from March to the end of June.

Detroit: An early variety that has been popular for the last hundred years. It produces good-sized beetroot with red, very sweet fruits. Sow from March to the end of June.

Carrots The first carrots were yellow; they were bred to be the orange colour we know now by the Dutch in the sixteenth century in honour of William of Orange. These orange carrots had a higher sugar content than their yellow counterparts, and so were sweeter. They also contain high levels of carotene (vitamin A), and what child has not been told that eating more carrots will make them see better in the dark? They are said to have some anti-cancer properties and are also recommended to keep the skin looking young.

With celery and onions, the carrot is one of the 'Trinity' and the base of much Italian cooking, especially for sauces, ragùs and sughi.

CRUNCHY CARROT LOAF WITH MUSTARD AND THYME
by Dan De Gustibus

MAKES 1 LOAF

250 g Allinson strong white bread flour
250 g Allinson soft grain strong white bread flour
60 g carrot, grated
3 tablespoons black mustard seeds
1 teaspoon dried thyme

2 teaspoons granulated sugar
2 teaspoons salt
1¼ teaspoons Allinson easy bake yeast*
1¾ tablespoons melted butter
260 ml warm water

PUT THE FLOURS, carrot, mustard seeds, thyme, sugar, salt and yeast into a bowl. Mix to a soft dough with the butter and water. Turn on to a floured surface and knead for 10 minutes. Shape as desired and put into an appropriate greased tin.

Leave to prove slowly until doubled in size.

Add a topping or glaze of your choice, if wished, and place in an oven preheated to Gas Mark 7/200°C and immediately turn the heat down to Gas Mark 6/200°C. Bake for 25–30 minutes. When cooked, the loaf should sound hollow when tapped on the bottom.

Breadmaker method: Put all the ingredients into the breadmaker baking pan in the order specified for your particular model (see manufacturer's handbook). Set to the 'Basic White' programme for the appropriate loaf.

*If you want your loaf to prove faster, use 2½ teaspoons (1 sachet) Allinson easy bake yeast.

'Travasa pa vin a la leuna nuovella'

NEVER BOTTLE THE WINE WITH A NEW MOON

Bollito con Salsa Verde alla Piemontese followed by Brodo Svizzero
BOILED BEEF WITH SALSA VERDE FROM PIEDMONT
followed by Swiss Broth

The reason that this recipe gives you a two-course meal is that, having made the main course of bollito (boiled beef), you will end up with the broth, which is used for the next course. Curiously, you eat the main course first and then the soup afterwards (just like fondue Chinois) with a raw egg stirred into it. The egg must be very fresh – not one that's been lurking in the fridge for a month, please. This is true winter food. The beef will be really tender and can be served sprinkled with large sea salt crystals, the salsa verde (called 'bagnet verde' in Piedmont), a good Barolo or other full-bodied wine and a rustic loaf of bread, cut thickly. Put olive oil on the table instead of butter.

When making the croûtons for the brodo, fry the garlic first in the oil but don't let it burn or it will taste bitter. Discard the garlic before frying the bread until golden but, again, not too brown.
SERVES 4

For the bollito
2 large carrots (Nantese)
2 medium onions (Dorato di Milano)
2 celery sticks (Dorato d'Asti), leaves on
800 g brisket of beef
6–7 black peppercorns
1.5 litres of water
1 bouquet garni
1 tablespoon salt
For the salsa verde
a good handful of flat-leaf parsley (Gigante di Napoli), chopped
2 hard-boiled egg yolks
1 small clove of garlic (Bianco Veneto)

1 small onion
1 thick slice of bread, crusts removed, soaked in wine vinegar
3 anchovies or 8 cm anchovy paste
salt and freshly ground black pepper
1 teaspoon sugar
olive oil
wine vinegar
For the brodo
1 stock cube (optional)
4 medium fresh eggs
chopped parsley
croûtons to serve, made from diced bread fried in olive oil flavoured with a clove of garlic

FOR THE BOLLITO, wash the vegetables, put all the ingredients into a large pan and bring to a simmer. Don't be tempted to trim the fat on the beef – it's needed and the broth will still be only about 2 per cent fat! When making all meat broths you will need to remove the scum that appears, which you can do with a tablespoon and a mug. It will take 5 minutes or so but the broth will be clearer and taste better, so it's worth doing.

When there is little or no more scum, cover, reduce the heat and simmer gently for 2 hours, stirring occasionally. It doesn't matter if the meat sticks out from the water a little, as being covered it will cook through, but if this is the case do turn it over during cooking.

Meanwhile, make the salsa verde by putting all the ingredients except the oil and vinegar into a blender and whizzing together until fairly smooth. Then add some olive oil and vinegar.

After 2 hours, check the seasoning of the brodo (broth). If it still tastes watery you can add a stock cube to lift the broth – preferably chicken, as beef will be too overpowering.

Cut the meat diagonally into slices and arrange on serving plates with the halved vegetables. Sprinkle some sea salt over the meat and then add some of the salsa verde.

Heat the broth through until piping hot and then spoon it into four bowls. Break an egg into each bowl, sprinkle some parsley on top and bring straight away to the table. The egg will half cook through (this is why they need to be really fresh) and remain half liquid. While the eggs enrich the soup it is also surprisingly refreshing, and I've never had a bowl unfinished. Serve the croûtons alongside the soup.

Carne in Selvaggina
GAME STEW

This mountain dish comes from Stefania Fabris, a family friend in Roasio. Soaking the meat in the wine for two days not only makes it tender but also enhances its flavour. Although the recipe calls for venison, you could use any game. The walnuts must be left whole, in the shells, and will impart a special flavour to the dish. Don't use too many juniper berries as they are quite perfumed and can easily overpower a dish. SERVES 4

4 venison steaks
1 red onion, chopped
3 whole walnuts
3 large carrots
1 celery stick

2 bay leaves
3–4 juniper berries
1 bottle of red wine
salt and freshly ground black pepper
polenta, to serve

CUT THE MEAT INTO LARGE CUBES and place in a bowl. Add all the vegetables, cutting them to fit into the bottom of the bowl if they are too big, bay leaves, juniper berries and seasoning and pour in the wine. Cover with cling film and marinate for 2 days, turning the meat each morning and evening.

Cook in a saucepan on a low heat for about 2 hours, stirring occasionally. After this time, set aside the meat and walnuts and blend the vegetables, wine and spices together to form a smooth sauce. Put everything back into the pan, cover and warm through on a slow heat.

Serve with polenta and with a good Gattinara or Barbaresco wine.

Carrot growing tips

Sow carrots 1 cm deep from March to July, but be sure to dig your soil well so that it is quite fine and friable. You should sow carrots directly into the soil where they are to grow because transplanting them from a seed tray into the ground can attract the dreaded carrot root fly, which will lay its eggs in the base of your carrots. This sometimes happens anyway when thinning out (to 5 cm between each plant). You can use some fleece to cover them, or protect them with a portable cloche, for example.

Nantese of Chioggia: This is a Nantes carrot, but from Venice (the Veneto region). It is a mid/early, medium-sized root with an excellent flavour.

Berlicum: A mid/late variety, mid length with good flavour and reliability.

Parisier Market 4: Paris is built on clay and over the generations this variety has adapted. You can hit your head against a brick wall only so many times before you change – hence this variety is round. This gives it some advantages: you can grow it in containers, it suffers much less from carrot root fly, it grows quickly. It is a nice carrot in its own right and is great for children.

Flakee: Sometimes called a Flak carrot, this is Dutch in origin and a very large, fat carrot. Late. This variety used to be widely available in the UK but has been withdrawn by most seed companies so it is quite hard to find. Harvest from July to the end of November.

Calade F1: Early. A hybrid variety. A fine carrot, heartless with a crunchy texture. The smooth cylindrical root has a good colour. The carrots are 15–16 cm with dark green, medium foliage. Sow from February to July, and in the autumn too in warmer climates. An excellent bunching carrot and a superb market variety.

Jaune de Doubs: A French variety from Doubs near the Swiss border. It was originally only given to animals, but is now prized for its colour and flavour.

Celeriac Many people are not that familiar with this wonderful vegetable, which has a taste of celery and which can be eaten raw or cooked. It is a bit of an ugly duckling, a rough and uneven bulb that is difficult to clean, but in my opinion definitely worth growing for its very good flavour.

Most people who have eaten it cite 'celeriac mash', which is a mixture of mashed potatoes and celeriac with butter and seasoning, and this is certainly an excellent way to try it – after all, the flavour of celery is both recognizable and popular.

CAPRICCIOSA

A good complement to summer foods and for picnics, this is quick and easy to make and will keep for a few days. The carrots will reduce the strong celery flavour of the celeriac and make the dish sweet, the ham will add saltiness and the mayonnaise creaminess. It goes especially well with salami, mortadella, prosciutto and other sliced meats. SERVES 4

1 medium celeriac
4 large carrots
3 slices of ham

mayonnaise
salt and freshly ground black pepper

THE FIRST THING TO DO is clean the celeriac, which is not always an easy task as their irregular shape makes them awkward to get into. You can use a potato peeler to take the skin off, but then use a paring knife to cut into any holes and properly clean it. Wash the celeriac to ensure it is fully cleaned, then scrape and wash the carrots too.

Grate the celeriac and carrots on the large holes of the grater and put them into a bowl. Cut the ham slices into small squares and put that into the dish along with enough mayonnaise to bind or coat the mixture, but not so much as to be either gloopy or runny. Season to taste.

WELL-DRESSED RAW ROOTS by Rose Prince

Four vibrant salads made from grated vegetables: parsnip and apple; beetroot; celeriac and broad bean; and swede. Eat them with charcuterie, boiled bacon or beside meat or fish terrines. I also like to eat these rich little salads, which the French call rémoulade, with other vegetables: a potato pie, or with a dish of broccoli and lentils. It's good food for feeding the masses. An electric grating attachment to the mixer helps enormously. Save washing-up time by making the beetroot salad last. SERVES 10 AS PART OF A MEAL

600 ml single cream

sea salt and freshly ground black pepper

For the parsnip and apple

2 medium parsnips, peeled and grated

3 crisp, fibrous apples (such as Cox's), cored and
  grated

juice of 1 lemon

leaves from 4 sprigs of flat-leaf parsley, roughly
  chopped

10 cornichons (baby gherkins), sliced into small
  rounds

For the celeriac and broad bean

1 large celeriac, peeled and grated

400 g broad beans, blanched in boiling water for
  1 minute, then pinched from their skins (or use
  frozen beans, which do not need blanching)

2 tablespoons capers, washed and chopped

leaves from 4 sprigs of tarragon, roughly chopped

For the swede

1 large swede, peeled and grated

2 carrots, scraped and grated

juice of 1 lemon

2 tablespoons unsalted shelled pistachio nuts,
  toasted in a dry frying pan, then chopped

1 teaspoon cumin seeds, toasted with the pistachios

For the beetroot

3 fresh, crisp beetroot, peeled and grated

leaves from 4 sprigs of dill

10 pink peppercorns, crushed

PUT ALL THE INGREDIENTS FOR EACH RÉMOULADE into separate mixing bowls. Pour 150 ml cream over each and mix well. If the salad is too stiff, add a little water. Taste each and add salt if necessary. Add black pepper to all except the beetroot. Refrigerate until ready to eat.

Celeriac growing tips

Celeriac can be sown quite early, from February until June, and harvested right up until the end of December. You should always sow it into seed trays, 0.5 cm deep.

Bianco del Veneto: Late. One of the best varieties in Italy, from Venice, the plant is medium sized with ample leaves and the bulb is large with white flesh.

Fennel What constantly amazes me about nature is that you can plant a tiny seed into what is essentially dirt, and a plant grows and gives you back a vegetable like fennel, which is made up of crunchy white sheaths with a strong aniseed flavour. Where does that aniseed flavour come from? This I can't explain, but I do find it absolutely miraculous.

Fennel is very good for the digestion and fennel tea also has excellent effects on the digestive system. My aunt told me once that they would eat it after giving birth to help them make milk, and, though probably not proven scientifically, it is one of those old wives' tales that is more than likely true and that people have been following for generations. I've also read that fennel can help with the menopause.

You can substitute fennel for the cardoons in the recipe for Cardi Piemontesi (page 141), if you like, for a very tasty dish.

Insalata di Finocchi
FENNEL SALAD

This is excellent served with roasted or poached salmon or trout, or cold fish or meat dishes in the summer. SERVES 4–6

1 kg fennel
extra-virgin olive oil
white wine vinegar

1 teaspoon whole-grain mustard (optional)
salt and freshly ground black pepper

CLEAN THE FENNEL BULBS and wash them carefully in running water. Divide the sheaths and cut each one into strips. Place in a salad bowl.

Make a vinaigrette of oil, vinegar, salt and pepper, according to taste, and dress the salad.

For a sweeter dressing, use balsamic vinegar from Modena, and for a stronger flavour, add a teaspoon of mustard to the dressing.

Trota in Cartoccio
TROUT IN CARTOCCIO

I have always lived in London, but every year without fail we went to visit family in Italy. There is a small stream called the Giara that goes past the house where my grandmother used to live. She was a lovely lady, my nonna Emilia. She had nothing, yet everything was mine and Marco's, and she loved her grandchildren with all her heart. But she would dread it when we went fishing in the Giara with nets and brought home hundreds of tiny little whitebait. She would spend hours gutting them, putting them in seasoned flour and then frying them. They were delicious and she could always, always make something out of nothing.

The water was freezing, even in summer, as of course it was just melted snow. We also used to catch trout by putting our hands under the rocks, where they would often hide, and literally tickling their tummies. I'm not joking. It really does work. They were delicious and this is how my wonderful nonna Emilia would cook them.

Remember that we have fabulous trout in the UK and so make sure you buy the freshest fish you can find, which should be firm to the touch and with shiny eyes. There are some variations to this recipe. For example, you can add some chopped leek to the fish parcels, so you have an all-in-one dish. Or you can use wild fennel or the feathery tops of Florence fennel. A dash of vermouth or Pernod in the parcels also works very well. SERVES 4

4 trout	*8 knobs of butter*
oil	*1 lemon*
4 tablespoons fennel seeds	*salt and freshly ground black pepper*

GUT THE FISH by cutting the stomach, scooping out the innards and then washing out the cavity.

Lay out four pieces of foil large enough to wrap around each fish, with the aim of making a small parcel by crimping the foil at the top. Brush a little oil on each piece of foil, so the fish won't stick, and then put a fish in the middle of each.

Next, take a tablespoon of fennel seeds and a knob of butter and smear this inside each trout. Cut the lemon into quarters, squeezing the juice on the outside of the fish, and stuff the rind inside. Smear another knob of butter all over the skin of each fish. Season inside and out and then close the parcel by gathering the edges and crimping the foil with your fingers. Make sure there is some room inside for the steam to circulate and that the parcel is tightly sealed, so that the juices mix inside and make a wonderful sauce.

Bake in the oven at Gas Mark 4/180°C for 20 minutes.

You can serve this dish either by opening the parcel and transferring all the contents to a plate, or by placing the parcel on the plate and allowing your guests to open the foil. First they will get steam, and then the aroma of the butter, fennel and lemon. Serve with bread and salad.

SEA BASS AND ROASTED FENNEL with Coriander, Tomato and Wild
Rocket Dressing by Chef Alex Beard

SERVES 4 AS A STARTER

1 bulb fennel (Montebianco)

60 ml extra-virgin olive oil

1 teaspoon coriander seeds

juice of ½ lemon

a bunch of wild rocket, finely chopped

1 courgette, finely diced

a sprig of coriander, finely chopped

1 tomato (Rio Grande), skinned, deseeded and
*   finely diced*

1 x 600–800 g sea bass, scaled and filleted, each
*   fillet cut in half on a diagonal*

salt and freshly ground black pepper

CUT THE FENNEL INTO EIGHT LENGTHWAYS, toss with the olive oil, salt, pepper and coriander
seeds and roast for 30 minutes at Gas Mark 4/180°C.

Meanwhile make the salad by gently mixing together the rest of ingredients (apart from the
sea bass) and seasoning with salt and pepper.

When the fennel is nearly ready, lightly fry the sea bass fillets for 2 minutes on each side.

Serve the sea bass on the fennel and drizzle the coriander flavoured oil around the plates.
Enjoy!

ROASTED TOMATO AND FENNEL SOUP by Chef Amy Hunt,
Oak and Glass

SERVES 4

1 kg tomatoes (Principe Borghese)

2 bulbs fennel (Montebianco)

extra-virgin olive oil

sea salt and freshly ground black pepper

coriander leaves

PREHEAT THE OVEN to Gas Mark 4/180°C.

Cut the tomatoes in half and place on an ovenproof tray. Slice the fennel and place on top
of the tomatoes. Sprinkle olive oil over the tomatoes and fennel and season with sea salt and
ground black pepper. Oven roast for 25–30 minutes.

Pour the contents of the tray into a large bowl and blitz until it forms a smooth soup. Place
the soup in a pan and heat it through. If you need to thin the soup, use some tomato juice.
Sprinkle with fresh coriander leaves and serve with crusty bread and butter. Yummy!

Fennel growing tips

There are two types of fennel, sown at different times of the year. The most common type is sown from March to May, but there is also alpine fennel, which is sown from June to August and which I find more successful. You are sowing it with heat and growing it into cold, so it will be less likely to bolt. Normal fennel, on the other hand, is planted with some cold and grown into heat, and mine invariably seems to bolt. But if you are a beginner at growing veg and want to grow fennel because, like me, you absolutely love it, then grow something else: fennel is really picky and, to be honest, difficult to grow! Honesty is the best policy at this point and I want you to be successful in growing your vegetables – so start with something else and graduate up to fennel.

Now doubtless I'm going to be contacted by loads of people who never have problems growing fennel, but this is where gardening can be so variable: what eight people find impossible, two find easy! What tends to happen with me is that I get nice plants that then tend to bolt and go to seed, so I don't end up with the bulb but I do get the wild fennel leaves, which I use with salmon steaks, and then I get the fennel seeds, which I use to make Porchetta – Roman pork stuffed with garlic and fennel seeds.

I do have very heavy London clay and fennel likes a light soil that is also fertile. As my garden is new, I'm going to have to add lots of organic matter and sand to lighten the soil but make it rich, and then I will sow my fennel 1.5 cm deep (leave 15 cm between plants) in the spring and again in the summer and keep my fingers crossed.

Mantovano: Mid/early variety. A vigorous plant with a hollow cane, producing a pure white bulb of good dimensions. Crunchy and perfumed, it is sown from spring to the beginning of summer.

Montebianco: Mid/late. 'Montblanc' alpine fennel. A large bulb, crunchy with meaty sheaths, and a vigorous plant. The leaves are intense green and the plant has a full cane.

Romanesco: Mid/early. The intense green leaves and full cane form a crunchy, large closed head that has a strong aniseed flavour yet is juicy. Sow from March to May.

Bianca Perfezione sel. Fano: Mid/early. The bulb is of a good size, pure white with half-empty canes. The sheaths are meaty, crunchy and juicy. Sow from March to the end of April.

Di Parma sel. Prado: A mid/late alpine fennel variety from Parma. The white bulb is compact with crunchy sheaths and a full cane. Sow from mid July to the end of August and harvest to the middle of November.

Okra I am not a big fan of lady fingers, as okra is otherwise known. I find it slimy and have never found a recipe for the vegetable on its own that I like, but if anyone wants to invite me to try it their way, I may just change my mind!

Zuppa Sarajevo
SARAJEVO SOUP

There are many dishes using okra that come from India and the Caribbean but this Franchi recipe comes from eastern Europe, where apparently okra is very popular. The use of soured cream is typical of the region. It is a rich and tasty soup that reflects the cultural past of Sarajevo, being a dish that both Muslims and Christians can eat. SERVES 4

30 g butter

300 g veal, cubed

80 g mixture of chopped carrot and onion

30 g flour

50 g okra, chopped

2 egg yolks

50 ml soured cream

chopped flat-leaf parsley

salt and freshly ground black pepper

MELT THE BUTTER IN A SAUCEPAN and fry the cubes of veal together with the carrot and onion on a medium heat for a few minutes to seal the meat. Add the flour and stir so that everything is coated, then add the chopped okra and season to taste. Cover with water and bring to a gentle boil, skimming the soup just as it starts to simmer. Simmer for 30 minutes.

Just before serving, test the soup for seasoning and adjust if necessary. Mix the eggs and the soured cream together.

Remove the soup from the heat and leave for a minute before stirring in the egg mixture. Alternatively, put the sour cream and egg mixture directly into each bowl as you serve. Sprinkle with parsley and serve with bread for a filling meal in one bowl.

Okra growing tips

Okra is a tropical vegetable that requires heat. It is possible to grow it from seed, but you must do so in a heated greenhouse or polytunnel. Sow 1 cm deep and about 50 cm apart when the temperature is at least 15°C. Harvest until the weather changes for the worse.

Clemson Spineless: Early. This variety forms a good bush and produces well. The fruits are of medium length, tapering, with green skin and white flesh.

When I originally saw this picture from the Franchi archives, I thought the ladies were just filling the seed packets.
In fact, they are actually selecting the best seed, almost one by one, by hand, removing any impurities.

Salsify We tend to associate salsify with France, and I have to say that up until about two years ago, we found it very hard to sell. Then Gordon Ramsay used them on the F Word programme and now everyone wants to grow them.

Salsify has a unique flavour with a slight taste of oyster, and can be used in stews, casseroles and soups. It will melt into a stew in the same way that a carrot or potato will and so both enhance the flavour and make it thicker and more substantial. Salsify is also very nice just boiled and served with butter, or dressed with olive oil and Parmesan.

To prepare them, you should scrape the skin off and then throw them into acidulated water (either vinegar or lemon juice will do) to prevent them going black and discolouring. Then they are ready to use.

Salsify growing tips

Vegetables are not immune to fads and fashions and, both before and after the Second World War, salsify was grown in the UK. The reason for its decline is probably because it grows very long at about 25 cm or more and so it is quite a pain to dig up. It is a real winter vegetable in the sense that it is sown in the summer and, having matured by November, it can be left in the ground until March or even April.

There are two main types, white and black, but they should both be sown 2 cm deep from March or April to the end of July.

White salsify: White is the type we tend to refer to as 'vegetable oyster'. It looks a bit like a parsnip but is longer and thinner. In Italian it is called scorzabianca, literally 'white skinned'. It has blue flowers, and the young leaves can be eaten raw in salads.

Black salsify: This type is still called by its Italian name in the UK: scorzanera, or 'black skinned'. It actually has Russian origins and the main variety is Géante Noire de la Russie. This one doesn't taper as much as scorzabianca, tending to be the same size all the way down.

Spinach For me, spinach is one of the nicest of all vegetables, and a very versatile one too. You can eat it raw (washed carefully) as young leaves in salad, you can boil it and make creamed spinach, you can use it in a wide variety of dishes from filled pasta with ricotta to quiches and tarts, and it's full of iron. It even had a cartoon based upon it. In Italian, Popeye is called Braccio di Ferro, or Iron Arms, because when he ate the spinach, his arms would explode with rippling muscles.

What always amazes me is how much water there is in spinach. If you are serving it boiled, you really have to squeeze the leaves out first, otherwise you will get a puddle of water on your plate.

Tortelli di Spinaci
SPINACH TORTA

My zio Tony's spinach torta is legendary and a speciality of Borgo Val di Taro where his family hails from. It's true that the simplest ingredients and recipes often make really tasty dishes loved by everyone. This is a great picnic dish also. Although this version doesn't call for pine nuts, you can toast some to taste and add to give a nutty flavour to the torta. SERVES 8

4 handfuls of fresh spinach	a handful of pine nuts (optional)
60 ml olive oil	grated Parmesan cheese
3 cloves of garlic, chopped	500 g puff pastry
1 large onion, chopped	3 eggs, beaten
6 fresh basil leaves, torn	salt and freshly ground black pepper

WASH THE SPINACH and blanch in salted water for 2 minutes. Remove, drain and squeeze out as much water as you can.

Pour the olive oil into a pan and gently fry the garlic, onion, fresh basil and pine nuts, if using, mixing in the spinach after a few minutes and adding a generous amount of Parmesan, salt and pepper. Fry for just a few minutes over a medium heat and then switch off the heat, leaving the ingredients in the pan to warm through.

Roll out the pastry to about 3 mm in thickness and use it to line a greased shallow ovenproof dish, allowing an overlap of 2 cm round the edges.

Spread the spinach filling inside to about 1 cm in thickness, then pour the beaten eggs in on top and fold the pastry to overlap the edges of the spinach to seal it.

Bake in the oven at Gas Mark 4/180°C for 40 minutes and serve hot or cold.

Spinach growing tips

Spinach is very easy to grow and it matures quickly too. Like many vegetables, it hates the heat and will bolt or go to seed if it is too hot. It really likes cool or cold weather and that is why you tend to sow spinach in the autumn and the spring, but not usually in the summer, although there are always exceptions. There are two main types of spinach: smooth leaf and blistered leaf. Smooth-leaf spinaches tend to have a meatier leaf and so they are better for cooking and not so good for eating raw. Blistered-leaf spinach, on the other hand, is very tender and superb for eating raw, but you can also cook it.

Riccio d'Asti: Small to mid-sized, roundish, blistered, intense green leaves from Piedmont. The leaves are very tender and suitable for eating raw or cooked. Sow from February to May and from September to October.

America: Mid/early. It is said that this variety was brought to America by Italian immigrants who carried the seed in their pockets. So, whenever anyone referred to the variety, they would say 'America, America', and the name stuck. A blistered-leaf spinach, the compact plant has firm leaves that are tender to eat. Sow from February to May and from August to October.

Merlo Nero: 'Blackbird'. A nice, tender, open-pollinated spinach from Italy. Sow from February to April and August to October.

Viking: Mid/early. A smooth-leaf variety with wide, thick, tender leaves. It is suited to autumn and winter cultivation. Sow from February to May and from August to October.

Gigante d'Inverno: 'Winter Giant'. A very large upright spinach with smoothish leaves. Recommended for autumn and winter harvest. Sow from February to April and August to October.

Lorelay: A mid/late spinach, semi upright and of good dimensions. The leaves are rounded, only slightly blistered, thick and consistent. It has good resistance to heat, so can be sown from the end of summer for an autumn/winter harvest or in spring for a summer harvest.

Andhalù: A Spanish variety. The plant is full, round and upright with short, small to mid-sized, light green leaves. An excellent variety for cooking, especially with ricotta, and general use. Sow from February to March and September to October.

7R F1: A professional variety, early, vigorous and very productive. The head is of good dimensions, firm with slightly blistered leaves. Sow from February to April and from August to October.

Scenic F1: From the Franchi professional range, this is a vigorous producer, both in spring and autumn. It has semi-blistered, tender leaves of intense green. Sow from February to April and from August to October.

Swiss Chard Swiss chard is related to the beetroot family, and the names are very similar in Italian: chard is 'bieta', beetroot is 'bietola'. That is why there are red- and pink-legged varieties and the flavour is quite earthy. It is a good source of vitamins C and A.

It is a vegetable that gives you two different uses: you have the lovely meaty stalk, or leg, which can be blanched and then cooked with eggs and Parmesan, say, or simply tossed in a hot pan with some oil and then sprinkled with Parmesan; and you also get the big leaf, which can be used just like spinach.

Tortelli di Erbette
TORTELLI WITH RICOTTA AND GREENS

Making filled pasta takes some time, but the difference between it and shop-bought – well, there is no similarity. Swiss chard works particularly well with this dish because its earthy flavour is tempered by the ricotta, giving the tortelli a richer taste. You can use spinach if you don't have chard – spinach and ricotta are of course a mainstay of Italian cuisine. Do use green chard and not red, which will give the tortelli a funny pink colour when cut open. SERVES 4

For the filling
250 g Swiss chard tops
300 g ricotta cheese
1 egg
70 g Parmesan cheese, grated
a pinch of nutmeg
1 teaspoon salt
freshly ground black pepper

For the pasta
4 eggs
400 g durum wheat flour
1 teaspoon salt
semolina for dusting
olive oil
butter
grated Parmesan cheese and sage leaves (optional),
  to serve

MAKE THE FILLING FIRST and pop it in the fridge so that the pasta doesn't dry out. Blanch the greens in some slightly salted boiling water, then carefully but firmly squeeze them to remove excess water. Chop, and then gently work the greens into the ricotta cheese with your hands, along with the egg, Parmesan cheese, nutmeg, salt and pepper.

To make the pasta, mix the eggs, flour and salt together until you have a dough ball.

Dust it with flour, roll it out roughly by hand and put it through your pasta machine starting at the thickest setting and reducing each time to a medium/thin thickness.

Cut the pasta sheets into squares of about 6 cm and put about 1 teaspoon filling into the middle. I always think I'm putting too little in and am tempted to add more, but then they always burst. You can make bigger tortelli if you wish in order to save time, and 9 cm squares work well with a larger dollop of the filling.

Brush the edges of the pasta with a pastry brush dipped in a little water and place another pasta square on top, pressing down gently to seal the edges. You can 'tidy' the edges by trimming them with a pastry wheel.

Dust the pasta squares with semolina to stop them sticking and stack them on a plate between layers of greaseproof paper.

Bring a large pan of salted water with a teaspoon of oil added to the boil and simmer the tortelli for a few minutes (fresh pasta cooks very quickly).

To serve, divide into four bowls, add a knob of butter or good-quality olive oil and fresh Parmesan. You can also fry some sage leaves to taste and scatter these over the pasta.

Chard growing tips

It wouldn't surprise me if chard has Swiss origins, as Swiss chard will die back in winter and then, come the spring, even after the coldest weather, it pops up again as if by magic. The other advantage of Swiss chard over spinach is that it really doesn't bolt and so is ideal for harvesting through the summer. I tend to grow spinach then chard then spinach, and this has always been very successful for me.

Swiss chard has a long sowing season, from March to September. Sow 1 cm deep, leaving 5 cm between plants. It should be sown directly into the soil rather than started off in seed trays. When harvesting, just cut it and it will grow back again.

Rhubarb Chard: Early. The Italians regard it as an inferior variety gastronomically, but the colour is stunning. It is early, vigorous and productive; medium sized with characteristic red stalks that are tender and of medium thickness. Sow from February to July.

Verde a Costa Bianca: Mid/early. The most popular variety in Italy because it is considered to have the best characteristics. It has thick, meaty, white stalks and large green leaves that cook like spinach. Boil the stalks and toss in butter or add to a frittata. It is slow to bolt. Sow from March to the end of July and harvest until mid October.

Verde a Costa Verde da Taglio: Late. Light green, smooth leaves that are cooked like spinach. This variety can be harvested six weeks later than Costa Bianca. It grows again quickly after cutting. Sow from March to September and harvest until the end of November.

Lionne: Early. A French variety from Lyon not far from the Swiss border. It has ample light green leaves with large, very tender white stalks. Sow from February to July and harvest until the end of November.

HERBS

Herbs are amongst the most important and widely used plants, both in the kitchen and for medicinal purposes, and there are many detailed books on them if you're looking for real depth on the subject.

Here I want to cover the basics, some growing cultural information along with a little history. I recommend a book by Claire Riley of Fishbourne Palace (the largest Roman villa north of the Alps) called *Roman Gardens and Their Plants* because it covers how certain varieties arrived in the UK and the cultural uses at that time.

There are different types of herbs. Annuals are ones that you sow and harvest in the same year, and the classic example would be basil. Then there are varieties that are semi-woody perennials, which will keep on going all year, every year. Here you are talking about plants like sage, rosemary and thyme.

Basil This wonderful fragrant leaf deserves its own section without a doubt. The Romans were responsible for bringing basil to Italy through their excellent trading channels, and from there it eventually reached Britain. Basil is used a lot in Thai cookery but it is popular all over the world, from Delhi to Dulwich.

The Romans knew not to cut basil with metal as it reacts with the blade, turning the cut areas black, and that is why you should always tear basil. They also, in fact, never ate it, but gave it to their horses and used it to treat ear infections. The Romans had such a passion and love of food, yet I can't help thinking that they missed out big time on the basil.

Basil both grows and goes well with tomatoes, if you excuse the pun, and what could be better than a Caprese Salad (sometimes called Tricolore because it is the same colours as the Italian flag) of basil, mozzarella and tomato? Tomato and basil just go together like priests and wine, and tomato sauces without basil are just not the same at all.

PESTO GENOVESE

If you've never made pesto, do it just once in your life and you will be thankful that you did. It tastes like summer and is nothing like the stuff you buy in a jar. Pesto is quite easy to make and unforgettable eaten fresh. It can be used on pasta, bruschetta and as a delicious dip. It can also be bottled (small bottles are best).

2 cloves of garlic, peeled
3–4 bunches of fresh basil ('Genovese')
1 heaped tablespoon pine nuts, toasted
3 tablespoons good-quality olive oil, plus
    1 wine glass

3 tablespoons grated Pecorino cheese
3 tablespoons grated Parmesan cheese
salt

PUT THE GARLIC CLOVES, basil and pine nuts in a mortar and slowly start to crush, adding the 3 tablespoons olive oil, Pecorino and Parmesan, a tablespoon at a time.

When it has reached a thick, homogenous consistency, empty it into a bowl and dilute with a glass of olive oil, mixing well. Season.

When using the pesto for pasta sauce, dilute it with 1–2 tablespoons of the water that has been used to boil the pasta.

Basil growing tips

Basil originated in the East and although it thrives in the warmer parts of Italy and other Mediterranean countries and regions, it really hates the cold – the first whiff of a cold breeze and over it goes. This is why a lot of people don't have success with basil. My mum grows huge bunches of fragrant basil, yet I live around the corner and just cannot grow it as healthily or prolifically.

Basil can also be grown to obtain the essential oil, and experiments have found that basil grown in slight shade gave 137 per cent more essential oil than that grown in full sun. They also found that removing the flower heads as soon as they appear will increase the plant's life. In theory, you can sow basil at any time of the year as long as you give it the right conditions, which are heat, light and water. Generally, it is sown from March to July. It grows well alongside tomatoes, which is good partnership planting, helping to deter greenfly and attract beneficial insects.

I do three sowings of basil per year. The first, February to March, 1 cm deep, protected, in a pot, lasts me a couple of months. The second one I do outside in the ground in the summer when there are no more risks of frost, and the third one I do in a pot in September, bringing this in when the weather starts to turn cold. It works well, even though my basil-growing skills and my conditions are not ideal. I get a good crop and more than enough to make fresh pesto. My basil may not look so healthy, but it tastes really good.

Basil Genovese: Beware straight away, as it is now illegal to call basil 'Genovese' (i.e. from Genoa) unless it has been raised in a certain region of Liguria. This is because it now has an 'IGP' – Indicazione Geografica Protetta – which is a bit like a DOC on wines. Some suppliers of both seeds and plants are still flouting this ruling so be careful of what you are buying. Of course this is the classic variety for making pesto, but production of basil from this region is so small that it could not possibly produce enough to supply seed companies around the globe.

Classico Italiano: Classic 'Genovese'-style basil, grown outside the IGP area but still produced in Italy. This really is the classic, with many culinary uses.

Violetto Aromatico: I find that purple basils are a little fussier to grow than the green ones, but they are sweet tasting and, as food is about colour as well as flavour, these coloured varieties are much in demand. This particular variety has an aftertaste of cloves and a lovely deep red colour.

Bolloso Napoletano: Famous Neapolitan large-leafed basil with blistered leaves. In America, this outsells the classic 'Genovese'-style basil. It is so popular because the flavour is so outstanding, but in Britain it is hardly known.

Foglia di Lattuga: Literally translated as 'lettuce leaf' basil, the leaves are huge – bigger than your hand. They are milder, so while not great for making pesto they are excellent for wrapping and for ripping into salads. I recommend wrapping around mozzarella balls and drizzling with olive oil or around slices of Parma ham filled with Russian salad.

A Piccole Foglie: Small-leafed basil with a really strong and intense basil flavour. It can be used raw on salads but is quite overpowering, so is much better suited to cooking.

Greek (Bush) Basil: This is the type of basil that has really small, very strong leaves. Personally, I find them too strong to eat raw, but I will concede that they make really 'basily' sauces! The plant forms a round bush.

Red Rubin: Mid/early. A vigorous plant with reddish purple and strongly scented leaves. Easy to cultivate and ideal for containers.

Thai Siam: An early and rustic variety used regularly in Thai cooking. It has highly perfumed medium-sized leaves with purple flowers.

Largo Dolce per Vasi: This translates as 'large, sweet, for containers', which pretty much says it all. A mid/early and rustic variety.

Alla Canella: Cinnamon basil is mid/early and, again, a rustic plant. The green leaves are tinged with violet and it is quite a sweet variety.

Al Limone: Lemon basil. Early. An old-fashioned variety, which goes particularly well with mozzarella. The plant is quite upright and the leaves are light green.

A Palla Verde Scuro (Bascuro): Bascuro is a bush basil with very dark leaves (scuro means dark). It is also a very highly scented variety and excellent for use in sauces.

Other herbs Although basil is the quintessential Italian herb, rosemary, thyme and parsley are just some of the many other herbs used every day in Italian kitchens.

Anguilla in Coccio al Forno
TERRACOTTA OVEN-COOKED EELS

This is a Venetian recipe and eel is eaten widely in the whole Veneto region. My mother-in-law in Tulse Hill cooks it occasionally but is finding it more and more difficult to obtain eels in Britain, the home of the jellied eel – which alas is a tradition almost lost. SERVES 4

800 g eel (preferably river eel with a white stomach)
2–3 cloves of garlic, chopped
a sprig of rosemary
2 bay leaves

a bunch of parsley
a handful of thyme
1 glass dry white wine
1 glass extra-virgin olive oil
salt and freshly ground black pepper

ASK YOUR FISHMONGER to gut and prepare the eel for you. Wash and dry it carefully. The original recipe calls for the eel to be cooked for about an hour in a metal pan on dying embers. You can put a little oil in a pan and cook the eel on a medium heat for about 10 minutes, then turn down the heat and continue to cook for another 45 minutes, checking from time to time to make sure it doesn't overcook or burn.

Transfer the eel to a suitable terracotta dish. Cover with the garlic, herbs, white wine and oil and season. Put into a medium oven, Gas Mark 3/170°C, for about an hour (a wood oven is traditionally used). When the meat is pure white, the eel is ready to be served in slices, accompanied by white polenta.

Uova Ripiene alla Piemontese
PIEDMONTESE STUFFED EGGS

I love these simple antipasti, which my aunt Angelina in particular makes so well – but never enough of course. In Piedmont, antipasti is our ruin anyway, and most people have a good repertoire of starters.

First, the eggs. Angelina once looked at the expiry date of some eggs I had bought at the supermarket and said: 'Eggs should be treated like meat. You wouldn't eat week-old meat, would you?' Of course she has been used to collecting her eggs daily for the last 70 years. My point is that you should buy free range, or barn eggs at worst, and use them as fresh as possible. Or get a couple of chickens like I did. That way, you'll have fresh eggs daily and you'll know what you've fed them and how they've been looked after.

You don't have to include tuna in this recipe. I have had these eggs with and without, and they were both nice. SERVES 4–6

6 hard-boiled eggs

2 tablespoons chopped fresh parsley

1 teaspoon capers

3 anchovies, chopped

2–4 tablespoons olive oil

2 teaspoons white wine vinegar

1 tablespoon mayonnaise

2 tablespoons canned tuna, drained

salt and freshly ground black pepper

A LITTLE IN ADVANCE OF SERVING, you will have to boil the eggs. Delia Smith is still the authority if you want to know how long to boil an egg as she is a superb technical cook. Her *Complete Illustrated Cookery Course* was the first cookbook I ever owned and the basis for my home training! Delia says to place the eggs in cold water and bring them up to a gentle simmer. Then to boil size 4 eggs for exactly 6 minutes and larger size 1 and 2 eggs for 7 minutes. I find this works to perfection.

You can't peel warm eggs, so that is why you need to do them a little earlier. Put them under cold running water to speed up the cooling process if necessary.

Once shelled, cut the eggs in half lengthways and remove the yolks into a bowl. Add all the other ingredients and mash with a fork until you have a stiff mixture. If it is too gloopy and hard to mash, then just add a little more olive oil (or the oil from the tuna is also very nice).

Then simply spoon the yolk mixture back into the whites and serve with sliced meats like prosciutto di Parma, prosciutto cotto, bresaola, speck, salame or mortadella.

Sciroppo di Menta della Lina
LINA'S MINT SYRUP

Lina is an old lady in my village in Italy who knows all the local traditions. I call her when I want growing tips, but especially preserving tips. This is one of her recipes and is how it's been done in her family since she can remember. Shop-bought mint syrup is bright green, but this is the real thing, and the colour and taste will be natural and delicious and thirst-quenching on a summer day.

You can also use the syrup as an ingredient for cocktails or as a vodka mixer, or in cooking, for example to flavour icing or to soak into sponge cakes.

You can try the same basic recipe with other herbs – lemon balm works well – or add blackberries and other fruits during the infusion stage to further colour and flavour the mixture to your liking.

2 bottles of white wine
750 g granulated sugar
4 large handfuls of fresh mint leaves

FIRST YOU HAVE TO MAKE THE SYRUP. Place the white wine in a saucepan with the sugar and gently bring to a simmer, stirring often until the sugar has completely dissolved. You may find some scum forms on the top of the syrup – remove this with a spoon. Allow to cool completely. Pour the cold syrup into a large, wide-necked jar and add the washed mint leaves. Place the lid on the jar. Turn or gently shake the jar every morning for 5 days to assist the infusion.

On the fifth day, remove the mint leaves and decant the mint syrup into bottles. It doesn't need to be refrigerated once bottled as the alcohol and sugar will preserve the syrup, but make sure you put a tight cork or seal into the bottle so the ants don't enjoy it too!

To drink, mix some of the syrup (to taste) with cold water and add a mint leaf.

When my dad first arrived in England he went straight to Piccadilly Circus – a famous landmark from many films. This is a typical photo of a newly arrived Italian wearing dark glasses and looking cool.

Coniglio della Nonna Emilia

NONNA EMILIA'S RABBIT

My grandmother made the best rabbit, which was dispatched, prepared and cooked the same day. Rabbit has gone out of fashion in the UK, yet they have excellent flavour, with very little fat, and are abundant.

This reminds me of something that happened the other day. I was watching Saturday morning TV with my little boy. On ITV people were pouring custard over each other – immensely funny, of course. I switched over to RAI and there was a cooking programme on, *La Prova del Cuoco*, for eight- to twelve-year-olds with lots of dancing and singing (songs about vegetables). The chef was making pasta with fresh squid and courgettes. He gave clear instructions to the children on how to clean the squid, and when the dish was finished he told them which wines would suit it best. The next dish was rabbit and the ingredients were 'fresh'. Again, the children were shown exactly how to prepare the rabbit and, at the end of the show, they all enjoyed the meal. A true demonstration of the Italian high regard and respect for what food is.

This is another recipe that is very simple and requires no tricks, just a good-quality fresh rabbit, not one that has been hung. SERVES 4

1 kg fresh rabbit	*a sprig of rosemary*
4 tablespoons flour	*1 glass white wine*
100 ml olive oil	*salt and freshly ground black pepper*

CUT THE RABBIT UP INTO PIECES using a chopper or heavy knife, hitting the back of your knife with your palm to cut through any thicker bones. Once you have portioned your rabbit, put it into seasoned flour. It won't coat the rabbit completely, but is enough to colour it well and make a good sauce.

Next, pour the oil into the pan and heat until it sizzles when you put the rosemary in. When it does, add the rabbit portions, being careful not to overcrowd the pan, and fry the rabbit until golden brown on both sides, which will take about 20 minutes over a medium heat.

Finally, add the white wine and reduce it slightly. You can remove the rabbit at this stage but I don't, as the wine cooks into the rabbit and flavours it even more. If leaving the rabbit in the pan don't turn it over when you add the wine, as one side will soften and the other will remain crisp.

Serve with mashed potatoes and white wine.

MILANESE SCHNITZEL OR ESCALOPES

Or, if you are in Bolzano, Schnitzel, by which name it is more commonly known in the UK. I remember as a child often having a plate of spaghetti with a Scallopina – the best of two dishes on the same plate.

I used to help Dad make hundreds of these each week in the deli and it was our speciality. We would make them fresh every day, cook them at 11.30, and serve them warm in an onion foccaccia roll with fresh salad and mayonnaise – and they were just the best. We always had a queue. Some customers would ask for the chicken to be heated; Dad always refused. 'It is crispy – if we microwave it, it will not be crispy any more and we will kill it.' Dad respected food more than these people and I never saw him heat one up for any customer!

The other good thing about Schnitzel is how far you can make them go. Two chicken breasts will feed four people as normal portions. They are also quite a summer dish, and are great for picnics. Good, simple, tasty. SERVES 4

2 good-sized chicken breasts
2 eggs, beaten
60 g grated Parmesan cheese
200 g dried breadcrumbs

vegetable oil for frying
a sprig of rosemary
salt and freshly ground pepper

LAY A CHICKEN BREAST out flat on a chopping board, remove the fillet and put aside. Cut the remaining breast horizontally into three slices. Place your hand on top and cut in a straight line with a sharp knife, bending down slightly to make sure you are cutting an even thickness. Repeat with the other breast.

Beat the slices and fillets out with a meat tenderizer so they are thin, but not transparent. This not only makes the meat more tender, but 'stretches it' so that it will go further. If you find the tenderizer sticking to the meat, just wet it a little now and then. Place the beaten-out slices in a bowl with the eggs, Parmesan, salt and pepper.

Pour the dried breadcrumbs into a tray or large plate. Lift an escalope from the egg mixture and put it into the tray of breadcrumbs. Now this is where many people go wrong. Their breadcrumbs don't stick to the meat because they are not rough enough! Take a handful of the breadcrumbs and cover the meat, then hit it with your fist or back of your hand, turning it and making sure the breadcrumbs are covering the meat evenly.

Heat the oil with the rosemary in a frying pan so that it sizzles when the escalopes are added, and fry three or four at a time until they are golden but not brown or they will become tough. As they are ready, remove them with a fork, dripping any excess oil back into the pan, and place them on some kitchen paper on a plate before transferring them to a serving dish. I would always serve a nice crisp white wine with Scallopine.

Other herb growing tips

ANISE Anise is mainly grown in Italy, Greece, Spain and France. It is used principally to flavour desserts, cakes and liqueurs, but is good in a whole host of other dishes too, including meat and fish. In 1905, Dr Giuseppe Ghetti, in an article in *Italia Agricola*, stated that anise likes a well-fertilized soil and that it performed better with man-made fertilizers rich in potassium, calcium and nitrogen than with horse manure.

The best time to sow is from March and during April, but it can be sown to the end of May. There are many varieties and they are all different. The anise from Romagna is the most common, but the one from Puglia has larger, rounded leaves, while there are also other good varieties from Albi, Russia, Malta, Tours and Anjou in France and Alicante.

BORAGE Use the edible flowers to decorate fruit salads, punches and port. The leaves, which have a flavour similar to cucumber, are good in salad. Various countries have different cultural uses; in the UK we typically put it in Pimms. Sow from March to the end of July.

CHERVIL A herb associated particularly with France, chervil can be used fresh, dried or frozen in salads, soups, sauces and with eggs, particularly in omelettes.

The leaves look like a light green parsley leaf and the plant is upright, reaching only about 40 cm in height. Sow 1 cm deep from March to the end of September.

CHAMOMILE COMUNE Chamomile is very popular as a bedtime drink in Italy, where young and old drink it regularly. Cultivated chamomile gives bigger flowers with a stronger fragrance than the common chamomile you see growing in alpine fields. So much so that 100 kg of the common chamomile will yield just 150–300 g essential oil, while that quantity of the cultivated variety would yield 800–1000 g oil.

People often remark that the tea they make from the dried flowers is bitter. The traditional way (and I know it works, because this is how I do it) is to always pull the whole plant up in July (if planted in March) and hang it upside down in a dry and airy place (a barn or shed, for example), then pick off the flowers once they are dried. Sow from March to the end of June.

CHIVES The mild onion flavour makes chives ideal for delicate dishes where the flavour of an onion would be too strong. A potato salad without chives would just not be right, and they also go very well with eggs in quiches and tarts and with black summer truffles.

If your chives go yellow and sad-looking in the rain, just chop them right back and they'll grow green and strong again. Increase chives by dividing the clumps in spring or autumn. You can bring some inside for winter use by potting them into a container at the beginning of November and keeping them at room temperature. Sow from February to the end of June.

GARLIC CHIVES As above, but with a flavour between garlic and onion, again making them an excellent addition to dishes where a milder flavour is required.

Sow from February to the end of June.

CORIANDER Both coriander leaves and the seeds can be used. Associated with India in particular, it is a versatile herb, which can be used in curries, with eggs, in soups and in many other dishes. Coriander has been used in Italy for centuries as a result of trade. Interestingly, the seeds were used to flavour jams and liqueurs. Coriander prefers a light soil and full sun and doesn't require any fertilizers. Sow from March to June.

DILL A very easy herb to grow, which goes with all fish superbly but with salmon like no other herb. It is used a lot in Scandinavia, most notably to make Gravadlax, and in Eastern Europe, and to be honest we should use it more too! Sow from March to June.

ERBA STELLA Buck's horn in English but not a very popular or well-known herb. It is eaten raw in salads, and the dried leaves can also be used to make teas. Sow from March to June just under the soil and space out to 10 cm per plant.

GARDEN BURNETT A little-used herb which is easy to grow and reaches 45 cm in height. The intense green leaves are upright and are picked young to use in salads. They have a mild cucumber flavour and are also excellent served with Pimms.
Sow from mid March to the end of June.

LAVENDER SPIGA Common lavender is considered a herb in Italy, although in reality it is used more for its wonderful essential oil than to flavour dishes. English lavender is one of the best in the world but the lavender produced in Piedmont in the alpine regions of Cuneo, Pinerolo and in the Susa valleys is also of exceptional quality. You can use the dried flowers to flavour sugar, biscuits and pork, but do be sparing. It takes 100 kg of flowers to yield 600–1000 g essential oil. Sow from mid February to the end of September.

LEMON BALM This is one of the ingredients used in the liqueur Chartreuse from Grenoble, in cologne and in the famous Aqua di Melissa from Italy. The leaves have a bitter-sweet lemon flavour. It is lovely for using in fruit salads and for making tea, and it aids digestion. The plant often seeds itself and is very easy to cultivate. Sow from March to the end of July.

LOVAGE In Italy, the variety is *Levisticum officinale* and is known commonly as 'mountain celery'. It has a strong celery flavour with leaves like flat parsley or celery. It is very good with eggs but is also used in soups and stews. Sow from February to June.

MINT One mint plant is enough for a home veg plot, and don't plant it into the soil because it will spread and you will never ever get rid of it once it establishes. Instead, either sow it in pots or plant the whole pot into the ground. Tradition calls for mint to be harvested in August when the plant is in full flower, always in the morning and never in the heat of the day, but you can use it by just picking the leaves when you need them. Sow from March to May.

OREGANO The essential ingredients on all pizzas and excellent on all breads too, this semi-woody plant produces small to medium-sized leaves which have a strong flavour that doesn't fade with cooking and dry well too. Oregano used to be called 'acciughero' because it was mainly used to flavour anchovies ('acciughe'). It is a perennial, so will always be there when you need it. Sow from March to the end of August.

PARSLEY Parsley is indispensable in Italian cuisine and is used in very many dishes, especially with fish and seafood, with eggs and anywhere you would use garlic, to temper the strength.

Parsley Comune 2: Common flat-leafed parsley. Parsley is pretty hardy and should keep going most of the winter. As I write this in London, in March, I have had my parsley outside all winter and the cold has not touched it. After cutting, it will grow back again. Parsley is slow to germinate at around 21 days. Sow from March to the end of September.

Parsley Gigante of Napoli: Neapolitan giant flat-leaf parsley that has larger leaves than the Comune variety and a really superb flavour. Sow from March to the end of September.

Parsley Riccio 2: Moss-curled parsley is not used as much in Italy because it is felt that it has an inferior flavour to that of its flat-leaf cousin. It is used for garnishing. Sow from March to mid October.

PEPPERMINT There are many different types of mint but this is the type most used in Italy, primarily in Piedmont and in Pancalieri in the north, together with 'green mint' ('menta verde') from Rome. There is also a large mint production in Hungary and Japan. All my Italian reference books say that England is the best place for mint, which of course it is, and it is no accident that there are many sweet manufacturers based in the UK who were among the first to use mint in confections.

Use mint leaves to make mint sauce for lamb (chopped mint leaves, sugar and spirit vinegar essentially), in fruit salads, taboulleh, punch and many other dishes. Peppermint leaves can be used to make mint syrup or dried to make tea, which is a decongestant and aids digestion.

ROSEMARY Rosemary was cultivated commercially at the turn of the century in Dalmazia (Isola di Lesina) and in the Alpes-Maritimes region of France. It is ideal for flavouring roasts, especially lamb and chicken.

The old Italian word for rosemary was 'ramerino', which translates as 'little branches', from its woody, branched plant habit. It prefers full sun and very dry conditions, and in the wild it is found in the Mediterranean region, on slopes, on the coast at low levels and anywhere where you could find thyme or lavender. Rosemary is most perfumed and aromatic when picked in June and July. Sow from April to mid July.

RUE A poor plant that will grow in stony and poor soils exposed to full sun. The leaves are described as piccante or spicy; they are bitter and strong in flavour. They are used to flavour grappa and other distillations. It was once believed that rue was one of the herbs used to flavour cognac, as its aroma was similar, but this is not true. Sow from mid February to the end of August.

SAGE I think sage is at the same time one of the most Italian of herbs and one of the most English of herbs. In Piedmont, we pick the leaves, wet them and dust with a little seasoned flour before pan-frying them in olive oil and then serving them with Martini, our local aperitivo. But in England, I love pork and sage stuffing. Then in both countries there are beef olives, or involtini, where a sage leaf is rolled into a fine slice of beef and then fried.

After sowing from seed, the first year you can expect to harvest 100 g of leaves per plant, the second year 200 g and the third year 250 g. A wonderful oil called Olio d'Ambra is made with sage flowers, but it is very expensive because you can only obtain a maximum of 1 g of this essential oil from 1 kg of the flowers.

Sage grown in drier conditions gives a much better flavour and bigger yield, so plant it in the corner of your rockery in shallow soil and in full sun. Sow from mid March to the end of September. Sage should not be grown for more than four years in the same spot.

SCUPLIT This is a bit of an oddity and is not even that well known in Italy, which is the only country where I have ever seen it. Its Latin name is *Silene inflata*. It has a sweet flavour and the leaves are added to enhance salads, soups, omelettes and risotto. This rustic plant is very easy to grow. Sow from March to the end of June.

SENAPE BIANCA Use the small leaves for their mustard flavour in salads and pasta with cream. (The ingredient used to make mustard is Black Mustard). Sow from March to June.

SORREL Sorrel can be cooked like spinach and grows fairly easily. It can also be added to lamb, beef and omelettes and used for making soups. We supply some outlets in certain areas of London that sell out of this variety weekly, such is the demand in those areas. Sow from March to the end of June.

SUMMER SAVORY A little-used herb which is very nice cooked with both chicken and beans and is used commercially to flavour salami. It is widely grown in Piedmont, where it is called 'erba cerea', and it is used to flavour vermouths, which are very popular in Turin and Milan especially.

It prefers hot and sunny positions and a light or even sandy soil and originates from southern Italy. Sow from mid March to the end of June. Plants should be set 25 cm apart.

SWEET MARJORAM Add to meat dishes in the last few minutes of cooking, or to butter sauces for fish. Sow from mid March to mid October.

TARRAGON Tarragon was prized by the Arabs and was brought to Europe during the Crusades. In Italy, it first arrived in Tuscany before spreading to other regions, but it is associated strongly with French cuisine. The leaves have a mild aniseed flavour and it is superb with eggs, chicken dishes, pork and fish and is, of course, the main flavouring of Béarnaise sauce. My aunt told me that it was used locally to treat fever and stomach problems by infusing 20 g per litre of water to make tea.

Take care when making tarragon vinegar: if you just chuck some tarragon in some vinegar it will start to smell unpleasant. You need to first dip the leaves in boiling water and put them into the vinegar once they are completely dry. To make 400 g of essential oil, you need 100 kg tarragon. You can well understand why these oils are so expensive if you imagine the work involved in producing and harvesting 100 kg of tarragon!

French tarragon cannot be easily raised from seed and so Russian tarragon is the one usually sold in seed packs. If you want French, you really have to buy a plant. The plants reach about 50–70 cm in height and they don't much like very heavy clay soils. You can divide them so that one plant becomes two, setting them 50 cm apart. You can start harvesting the leaves as soon as you see them and each time you cut them, they will grow back sweeter and more tender in just a matter of days. You should replace tarragon plants every three to four years. Sow the seeds from March to the end of June.

THYME OF PROVENCE The best strawberries are British, the best cooking tomatoes are Italian and the best thyme is French – and in France the best thyme comes from Provence, where the conditions are excellent for growing both thyme and lavender, amongst other things. The very small leaves go well with both meats and fish.

Thyme is perennial, which means – like rosemary or sage – it is always there. Sow from March to the end of August.

WILD FENNEL Many of us who struggle to grow fennel, because it is so temperamental, end up with wild fennel, which is basically the fronds and seeds. These seeds have a really nice aniseed flavour and are the main seasoning in the Roman dish Porchetta, which is pork stuffed full of wild fennel seeds, garlic and rosemary and then cooked slowly until the meat is really infused and well flavoured with the fennel seeds. I also use them a lot with trout and salmon cooked in foil with butter and lemon. They can be used in sweets too and are excellent in rice pudding and biscuits, for example. Sow from March to the end of June.

tartufi e *funghi*

TRUFFLES AND MUSHROOMS

Truffles are essentially underground mushrooms and are considered to be the ultimate gastronomic experience. They don't look particularly appetizing, they are hard to find, have a short shelf life and are expensive to buy, but their flavour is, well, indescribable, in a good way. A very good way!

Just because I pick mushrooms, people think that I am an 'expert', knowing every mushroom and toadstool in the woods. But most mushroom-pickers know three or four varieties intimately and they only collect those.

Truffles I once tried to send my mum a text message to tell her with much excitement that I had found two whole, fresh white truffles. My phone has predictive text but the dictionary didn't include 'truffle'. I remember thinking, how on earth could such an important word be missing? After all, if I had my phone's weight in truffles, it would have cost me some hundred times more than the phone package!

The Romans knew all about truffles and appreciated them for their gastronomic value. There are Roman mosaics and frescos of men with pigs out truffle-hunting, and there are texts that also mention them.

Truffles are quite 'cloak and dagger'. You wouldn't believe what happens in certain parts of Italy if you go looking for these precious fungi where you shouldn't. I remember going truffle-hunting on a farm that had been set up by Raggi Vivai, the leading supplier of truffle trees in Italy. I had become separated from our group and was quite happily digging away in the ground when I heard a click and looked up to see the barrel of a shotgun pointing directly into my eyes. It was a farm hand who didn't know me and thought I was poaching, but when I nervously explained, he put the gun down. This is big business. Elisabeth Luard once told me that at the main truffle markets the women are all armed with pistols.

There are probably almost as many truffles in the UK as there are in Italy. No one really knows as they are not hunted much here, whereas in Italy most people would recognize an edible truffle in the wild. There are poisonous varieties as well as edible, and although these won't kill you, you don't want to find out, so if you come across a truffle in your garden, don't assume it's good to eat. And yes, people do find truffles when mowing their lawns in Kent or weeding in the Chilterns.

In 2003, truffle prices hit record highs and this trend has continued virtually every year. This was partly due to a lack of production, despite the fact that truffles are now being farmed successfully, even in the UK, and also because of a rise in demand. White Pregiato truffles hit £2000 per pound that year. Apart from the fact that they are found in only two places in the world, they also have a short shelf life of a couple of days. There is the famous story of the London restaurant that spent £20,000 on a white Alba truffle. They put it in the fridge and it rotted. And I feel bad when I forget a yogurt at the back of the fridge!

Fonduta con Tartufi

CHEESE FONDUE WITH TRUFFLES by Elisabeth Luard

If you can lay your hands on fresh 'magnato', ask three of your best friends to share the feast – as with a pound of caviar, four is the maximum number to one good-sized truffle. If necessary, you can replace the Fontina with half Gruyère and half Emmental cheese. SERVES 4

300 g Fontina cheese
300 ml milk or single cream
4 egg yolks
To finish
1 good-sized (30–50 g) fresh white truffle, cleaned

To serve
toasted country bread or plain risotto (or plain-
    cooked potatoes, boiled or baked)
unsalted butter

CHOP THE CHEESE INTO TINY PIECES with a sharp knife – worth the effort since it produces a smoother mix than if you grate it, but a food processor will do the job in no time.

Put the cheese into a basin with the milk warmed to blood heat. Stand the basin over a saucepanful of boiling water. Cover it with a clean cloth. The milk and cheese must be kept warm on the side of the stove for an hour, so that the cheese melts very gently into the milk. While you are waiting, make a plain risotto, or prepare thick slices of fresh bread for each of your guests. Put four plates to warm.

At the end of the hour whisk the egg yolks with the cheese and milk. Put the saucepan on the heat and bring the water to the boil. Turn it down to simmer. Carry on whisking while the mixture thickens over the simmering water. Don't hurry it. When the mixture has thickened so that it can comfortably blanket the back of a wooden spoon, take it off the heat.

Make sure your friends are all at the table, each with a warm plate on which you have placed either a thick slice of bread scattered with little pieces of fresh butter or a mound of risotto. Pour the fonduta over the bread or risotto, or hand the pan to the participants and let them serve themselves, along with the truffle and its grater.

Truffle growing tips

You wouldn't believe the number of times I have had hazelnut trees inoculated with truffle spores for sale on my stand at shows, and someone at the show is convinced that these trees will grow chocolate truffles. Honestly. It's so daft I couldn't even make it up. Although the prize goes to the lady who bought ten packs of San Marzano tomato seeds and rang to complain because she thought she was buying tinned tomatoes.

There are a few edible indigenous, native varieties in the UK, of which the Black Summer Truffle, often called the English Truffle, is the most common. The white truffle, *Tuber borchii*, is also native and is found in smaller quantities. None of the European truffles are found in America, but they do have their own truffle varieties not found here – the Oregon Truffle and the Pecan Truffle seem to be the main ones.

There are truffle farms in the UK, some of which we are responsible for setting up, and their locations are, for obvious reasons, a secret. There are more being set up that will be in production within a decade.

The general rule is the harder they are to find, the more expensive they are, and none is so rare as the White Pregiato truffle. This is because it is found only in Piedmont and Umbria in Italy, and will not grow anywhere else. To say it's fussy is an understatement, and beware of companies offering to sell you a truffle tree impregnated with this spore. Almost certainly it won't grow in your garden in Essex, but there are other superb varieties that will, believe it or not, and I'll come to those shortly.

French Perigord truffles are the best of the black truffles, often used, amongst other things, in fine French pâtés where a black vein runs through the middle of the meat. These too will not grow very successfully in the UK, and again their price reflects their limited availability.

The hazelnut bushes for truffle farms are grown in a sterile environment to avoid cross-contamination from competing fungi, and their roots are impregnated with truffle spores. The varieties we offer are found naturally in the UK, and so this gives them the best chance to succeed. Truffles are taken very seriously in Italy, and the plants are tested and certified by various bodies before being allowed for sale, to ensure quality and successful inoculation.

Truffles require three main conditions:
1. Soil that is not compacted (like a lawned area for example) – an unused part of the garden would be ideal.
2. Soil that has a PH between 6.5 and 8.5 (not acid).
3. Well-drained soil.

The plants are about 50 cm tall, will last 50–70 days and need little maintenance, growing very quickly at first. They can grow to 7 m tall if left, but can be trimmed into 2 m hedges and the nuts are edible. They will lose their leaves in the winter when dormant. Truffles can spread, although slowly, and don't harm other plants or trees.

Plant in either full sun or half shade. Make a hole large enough to take the plant, add some grit and remove any roots in the soil, which may carry competitive fungi species. Water in. No special care is needed other than to water for the first year during dry spells – in fact, it's best to leave well alone and let the roots develop. Never use fungicides and avoid tap water containing chlorine as chlorine kills fungi (eventually).

To harvest, carefully dig around the fibrous outer roots with your fingers and a stick, from just under the surface to 35 cm down, taking care not to damage the plant. Brush the truffles and refrigerate for up to 14 days, washing only prior to eating. Once washed, the truffle must be used up, preserved in oil or, better still, frozen, as it will rot quickly. A typical plant will produce about 50 g truffles per year on average after four to six years, and 80–100 g after 12 years.

It is worth pointing out that all truffle trees are sold as guaranteed as being capable of producing truffles when sold, but only if given the correct conditions. Don't forget that many things can happen to a plant in five years, from waterlogging or other adverse weather conditions to disease or cross-infection with another fungus, so it is not guaranteed that you will get truffles just because you planted one truffle tree. Also, if you don't find any truffles, it doesn't mean that the tree didn't produce them, just that you didn't see them when it did. The best way to find them is still using a truffle dog, even when you know where they are growing.

Black Summer Truffle/Scorzone: *(Tuber aestivum vittad.)* The easiest of all truffles for artificial cultivation. Scorzone truffles with eggs are famous. You can freeze them, grate the truffle into Parmesan cheese or into olive oil, and it is excellent with meats, pasta, potatoes or sauces. Walnut- to orange-sized truffles. A very good low- to mid-price truffle (30p per gram fresh). Harvest from June to September.

Bianchetto (or Marzuolo) White Truffle: *(Tuber borchii vittad.)* One of the easiest truffles to grow, tolerating a range of soils from sandy to clay. It has an intense perfume and flavour, and is wonderful used in frittata, mixed with mascarpone and spread on to bruschetta, shaved on to pasta, risotto or polenta and used to make truffle cream sauces. It freezes well. The pea-to apricot-sized truffles cost £2.40 per gram fresh. Small harvests are possible out of season, but its main harvest period is January to April.

Mushrooms I go for porcini and some other of the *bolletus* family, plus chanterelles ('gallidei' in Italian). The satisfaction of finding a good specimen – and eating it – is even greater than that of growing a vegetable, purely because of the thrill of the hunt. Sometimes you come away empty handed, and other times with baskets full. This is part of my culture, something special and indescribable. I must share this love.

There are some unwritten rules when collecting mushrooms, which unfortunately not everyone shares. I've heard of gangs being dropped off in woods where they pick everything they see. The mushrooms are then identified (hopefully properly) and sold to restaurants. The pickers have little or no knowledge, and certainly no respect for our forests.

This couldn't be further from the way proper pickers conduct themselves. I often bump into other Italian, Polish and Lithuanian families in the woods and we all show off our finds and genuinely admire each other's fruits.

Our rules are part countryside code, part military exercise and part common sense.
1. If you're not 100 per cent sure, throw it away.
2. Always cut mushrooms, never pick the whole thing. This leaves the spores so that future generations can flourish, along with the natural species that depend on them. Clean them there and then at the spot where you found them, removing any dirt either by cutting it off or with a soft brush.
3. Never, ever, tell or show anyone your spots! Mushroom spots are handed down from father to son and tend to reliably produce year on year. A general rule is to only show your spots to people you are willing to die for. If you meet fellow 'colleagues', send them in the wrong direction!
4. Never leave litter. If you have a picnic, take your rubbish with you.
5. Never shout with joy when you find something.
6. Don't put mushrooms in plastic bags. Use a basket. If you are in the fortunate position of finding more than you bargained for and need to use a plastic bag, line it with ferns.
7. Don't wash mushrooms (certainly not porcini or other bolletus varieties). You must clean them, of course, but this can be done effectively with a soft brush and wet kitchen roll.
8. If you come across one that you don't intend to pick, don't kick it over. How many rotted porcini I've come across in my life I cannot tell you, but it's heart breaking.
9. Never light fires in the woods.
10. Go at first light, or certainly as early as possible. This is one of the rules I don't always follow. My father-in-law goes at 5 a.m., but I work on the premise that the woods are big and even a pro can't find everything, so you will always find something if you go later. Besides, if you are taking kids, you try and wake them at 4 a.m. and see what happens.
11. Buy a proper mushroom knife (with a brush) or otherwise bring a pen knife. You really don't want to be stopped in the woods with an illegal weapon.

12. Wear boots, even if it looks dry.

13. Always take a phone or whistle to attract attention in case of accidents.

14. It's no accident that wild mushrooms are cooked with whole cloves of garlic. It is said that if the garlic cloves turn purple, you have a poisonous mushroom in the pan. This may or may not be true, but I don't wish to be the first person to find out, so it's advice I always follow!

15. Always cook mushrooms using wooden utensils, not metal.

16. Before you look down, you should look up! At the moon that is. No, this isn't old wives' nonsense: I can assure you that if it rains and there is a new moon, then you'll find mushrooms.

I didn't realize there was so much to it until I started writing the 'rules' out. Dad certainly did teach me a lot.

The way you deal with the mushrooms once you've found them and cleaned them tends to fall into three categories.

1. Eat straight away. These tend to be large porcini or bolletus mushrooms, which you would slice, dip in beaten egg with Parmesan and then into breadcrumbs, and fry until golden. This method is called impannata and is better than any steak.

2. Use for sauces or risotto. These tend to be mushrooms that are broken or damaged. Once you have eaten the head's impannata, the stalks can be used in sauces. You can freeze a good mushroom sauce or simply cook up the mushrooms with garlic and rosemary and freeze in blocks for use later on.

3. Preserve or put away.

Drying is an excellent way of preserving worm-eaten porcini and bolletus mushrooms, in particular. Slice the mushrooms longways so you have some stalk and head, place them on a wire rack, not overlapping, and pop them into the airing cupboard or near the boiler or a radiator, or in an oven with a bread-proving setting. You want to desiccate not cook them, and so you need a dry, airy place. Any worms will simply leave the mushrooms and die.

If you have been lucky enough to find small, healthy, perfectly formed and undamaged porcini mushrooms, then bottle them. You can also preserve larger porcini, as long as they are good quality. Cut them into 5 cm cubes. Bring to the boil enough white wine vinegar to cover the mushrooms, flavoured with a garlic clove, whole black peppercorns, rosemary and bay leaves. Boil the mushrooms for 20 minutes, then leave to drain before transferring to sterilized jars and topping with olive oil. Boil the jars for 10 minutes, allowing them to cool in the water before removing, in order to hermetically seal them.

They'll last at least a year in the larder and make the best antipasto. They are also excellent served on cocktail sticks, accompanied by a Cinzano or Campari soda.

Insalata di Funghi e Formaggio
MUSHROOM AND FONTINA SALAD by Camisa Deli, Soho

This would originally have been served with fresh white truffles. If you are lucky enough to have them, use another tablespoon of olive oil instead of truffle oil. SERVES 2–4

250 g hard white mushrooms (Prataiolo)

juice of ¹/₂ lemon

200 g Fontina cheese, rind removed

2 tablespoons extra-virgin olive oil

1 tablespoon truffle oil

salt and freshly ground black pepper

NOT MORE THAN 1 HOUR BEFORE SERVING, trim the stems of the mushrooms short. Wipe the mushrooms clean with some damp kitchen paper. Cut them into 3 mm thick slices, place in a serving bowl and sprinkle with the lemon juice to stop them discolouring. Cut the cheese into 1 cm cubes. Just before serving, add the cheese to the mushrooms, together with the olive oil, truffle oil (or fresh grated white truffle), and a pinch of salt and pepper to taste. Toss and serve.

Risotto ai Funghi
MUSHROOM RISOTTO by Camisa Deli, Soho

SERVES 3–4

75 g unsalted butter

1 large onion, finely chopped

50 g dried porcini, soaked in warm water for
*   30 minutes*

225 g fresh mushrooms, thinly sliced

1 glass dry white wine

350 g arborio rice

1 litre chicken or vegetable stock

3 tablespoons freshly grated Parmesan cheese

MELT 50 G BUTTER in a sauté pan and cook the onion over a medium heat, stirring often, until soft. Do not let it brown. Drain the porcini, straining the liquid through a sieve lined with kitchen paper. Rinse the porcini in cold water, chop roughly and add them to the onion with the fresh mushrooms. Cook, stirring, until the fresh mushrooms start to wilt. Pour in the wine and reduce over a slightly higher heat to 1 tablespoon. Reduce the heat to medium, add the rice and stir until the grains are coated. Add one ladle of stock, together with the porcini soaking liquid, and stir until the liquid is almost absorbed. Continue to add the stock, a ladle at a time, stirring often, until the rice is just al dente and the mixture is creamy. Do not let it stick to the pan. This will take about 20 minutes. If you run out of stock, add a little hot water. Turn off the heat, and put the remaining butter and the grated Parmesan on top of the rice. Do not stir it in, just cover with a lid and leave for 2 minutes. Finally, stir the risotto and serve with a bowl of grated Parmesan.

italiano essenziale

ESSENTIAL ITALIAN

Preserving This is a skill still used in Italy as part of both gardening and cooking, from making jams, pickles, mustards and sauces to salami and hams, cheeses and liqueurs. These will vary regionally, but even in the cities it's not uncommon for households to make their own sausages and cheeses as well as the 'normal' things like jam and pickles.

Throughout the war and after, as first the Germans and then the Allied advance took their toll on the infrastructure and resources, my family in Italy faced extreme hardship. But despite this they never went hungry because they knew how to forage for mushrooms, chestnuts, herbs and fruits of the forest. They grew vegetables, rice and corn for making polenta, they hunted wild boar, birds and other game, and they made their own wine and grappa. But more importantly, they knew how to prepare and preserve this bounty for later times.

DRYING This is the oldest way of preserving food for the winter months and is not always as easy as it sounds. You have to make sure that whatever you have 'dried' is actually properly desiccated. I dried some borlotti beans once, stuck them in a jar and found a week later that they were all mouldy. It's not hot enough in the UK to dry food in the sun, but there are other ways round this.

I have a food dryer that very slowly 'desiccates' the food using a mild heat and circulating air. It's not a cooking process, but one where the moisture, or much of it, is removed from the item in question. Another very good device is an Aga, and now a lot of modern ovens have a bread-proving setting at around 40°C, which, if used with the oven's fan, is ideal. The key is a mild, dry heat and a circulation of air.

It really isn't an exact science so be flexible with drying times. It can take 6–8 hours to dry tomatoes and there are many factors to consider. You must cut the tomatoes (or other ingredients) the same thickness, otherwise they will dry at different speeds and if not checked regularly some will become crisp and some will be undercooked.

Also, people like different things. I love sun-blushed tomatoes; my wife loves sun-dried. Sun-blushed are half dried and have a half-fresh/concentrated and half-dried flavour, but they don't keep so well, so you need to put them in the fridge or keep them in oil, whereas dried tomatoes can be kept at ambient temperature (or in oil).

Some great things to dry are mushrooms, shelling beans like borlotti and cannellini, tomatoes, figs, grapes, bananas (dry them until they are flexible and sticky rather than brittle – they are superb in cereal), plums and chillies.

FREEZING The modern way to preserve foods, but also used in ancient times in colder European countries and North America, where meats would be stored outside or buried in the snow to keep them all winter and prevent them from deterioration.

Some drawbacks of freezing are freezer burn and bad labelling of food, which sometimes leads to 'finding' an item in the freezer and not being able to remember when it was put there. Doubt creeps in and you end up throwing it away, just in case! Another potential drawback is a power cut. If you do have a loss of power, it is usually temporary. The one thing you should never do is open the freezer. Closed, your goods should keep frozen for at least 24 hours.

But the benefits far outweigh the drawbacks. Freeze borlotti beans rather than drying them and you don't have to soak them overnight before using them; they will cook in 40 minutes from frozen and 30 minutes from defrosted; and you can store them for about six months. Also, a frozen vegetable will taste more like the real thing than a dried vegetable that has been rehydrated by soaking in water.

Make sure that anything you put in the freezer is suitably and fully wrapped in freezer bags, cling film or a freezer-proof container. This will prevent freezer burn, drying out or other deterioration.

The other piece of advice is to freeze in portions. From working in the deli, I learned to do everything in portions, to the extent that I would look at a cake and in my mind would see six portions at £1.50 per portion! But what you don't want is to freeze ten servings of minestrone in a batch, and then when you need two you have to defrost the whole lot. Ice-cube trays work very well for freezing baby food, herbs and other small quantities. Separate larger items either into freezer bags (for example, for portions of chicken or vegetables) or into separate containers (for sauces and stock).

Also be sure to defrost properly, as you can really make yourself or your guests quite ill if you barbecue sausages that aren't thoroughly thawed. They will look cooked, but they will still be raw in the middle. The general rule is that the defrosted meat or vegetable must be soft all the way through; don't be afraid to test it by prodding with a sharp knife or by cutting the object in half. In an emergency you can finish off and speed up the process by using the defrost setting on your microwave, but I think using a microwave alone to defrost partly cooks and changes the flavour and characteristics of meat and vegetables. It's fine though to use the microwave to defrost stock and soups.

SMOKING This is a way to increase the shelf life of some meats, fish and cheeses, as well as change their flavour, by 'bombarding' them with smoke. This process cures the meat by a combination of the hot, dry atmosphere that the goods are exposed to for an extended period and the smoke itself, which has preserving properties. Some foods suit smoking very well – salmon, for example – and now that we all have fridges and freezers some foods are smoked just for flavour rather than for the preserving attributes. You can buy small smokeries for home use and a search on the internet should find you something suitable.

BOTTLING This is quite different from canning in that you can do it yourself at home. The possibilities range from passata to jams and preserves. Some things bottle really well, like gooseberries in Champagne, peaches in syrup or raisins in grappa and, of course, passata. Most bottled or jarred products will last about a year in the larder.

It's important to always sterilize jars before using them otherwise the contents might become infected by bacteria. Foods preserved in alcohol tend to be OK as the alcohol has sterilizing as well as preserving qualities, though you should still always use prime quality ingredients, apples with no bruises etc. In the case of jam, the boiling jam is put straight into the jars, and this will also act as an extra sterilizing measure as the heat will kill any germs. Putting the lid on will trap the heat and ensure that you have a hermetic seal. I normally heat the oven to Gas Mark ½ /100°C and pour boiling water over the jars before putting them to dry in the oven for about 30 minutes. Take care when taking them out as they will be very hot.

How to preserve foods in hermetically sealed jars
This is such a simple skill, but one that is seldom used these days. We would rather freeze things, or even throw them away, than preserve them in this way, yet many foods can be stored for up to a year in this way, and the jars are reusable and don't require electricity like freezers.

Place your ingredients into a jar with a suitable lid (although it's extremely practical to reuse jars, often the lids are very shallow and there is nothing worse when you go to boil the jars than water leaking in and ruining the contents). Seal the jars hand-tight only, place them in a deep saucepan and cover them with boiling water. If you don't have a pan that's deep enough, place a plastic bowl over the pan (making sure it doesn't burn on the gas), to trap the moisture and heat.

Put a tea towel in between the jars to stop them rattling and breaking against each other. Simmer for 10 minutes but do not remove the jars until the water has cooled. You will then have jars that are hermetically sealed.

Passata Fatta in Casa
HOME-MADE PASSATA

In Italy, San Marzano plum tomatoes are grown almost exclusively for making passata for the whole year. It's then stored in sterilized jars and used for pasta sauce, pizzas etc.

tomatoes (San Marzano 2, San Marzano Redorta or Roma)
about 1 teaspoon salt per jar
about 2 tablespoons olive oil per jar

DIP THE TOMATOES IN BOILING WATER to make removing the skin easier. Once peeled, push them through a sieve so that there are no seeds in the passata. Alternatively, you can buy a passata machine that separates the skin and pips from the pulp with a turn of the handle, which is infinitely quicker. You can flavour the passata at this stage with basil, chilli, thyme or whatever you like. Add salt to taste and place in sterilized jars.

The reason for adding both the salt and the oil is that, apart from flavouring the passata, salt is a preservative and the olive oil will form an airtight barrier on top of the jar, so add this last of all before sealing. Seal the jars following the instructions opposite.

ZIA ANGELINA'S GIARDINIERA

Aunt Angelina makes things in a traditional way, from scratch. She even makes the dried herbs and 'season-alls' she uses for cooking by harvesting each herb, chopping it, mixing with chopped garlic and salt and drying very slowly on her wood-burning stuffa (like an Aga). She makes ravioli stuffing from her livestock and vegetables, then she mixes the pasta dough and makes up the ravioli by hand. It's amazing that something that takes so long to make is polished off so quickly – but with a respect and pleasure that you wouldn't get with shop-bought pasta.

Her Giardiniera (of the garden) is a classic example of her dedication to doing things properly. She uses all her own vegetables if possible, and even the vinegar is her own as they also make wine and so have the madre (mother), a naturally occurring gelatinous substance used to 'turn' wine into vinegar, which can be used time and time again.

You make this wonderful side (which goes with any meats, charcuterie, eggs or just on its own with rustic bread and some wine) in five stages. It is important to cook the vegetable groups together as indicated below. This is the traditional way and it works.

3 kg tomatoes, cooked and processed using a passata machine or sieve, or about 2 litres ready-made passata
750 g carrots, 1 large head of celery
Chop the carrots and celery and fry together on a low heat for 30 minutes.

750 g French beans, 750 g pickling onions
Cook together, frying gently on a low heat for 30 minutes.

750 g courgettes, 750 g peppers
Chop and fry together on a low heat for 30 minutes.

a palmful of salt, 250 ml sunflower oil, 500 ml vinegar, 1 tablespoon sugar, 1 chilli
Boil these ingredients together for 20 minutes.

COMBINE THE INGREDIENTS and divide between jars. Seal following the instructions opposite.

Tomini Electric
CHILLIED TOMINI CHEESES

If you know Toma cheese, you'll know it as a medium to strong mountain cheese with an ash-black crust. But we also make fresh Tomini, which are mini Tomas that have a real tanginess and freshness to them. Then, and only in Piedmont as far as I know, we do this recipe which makes them 'electric' or hot by adding chilli. It is very simple and will work with any small whole fresh cheeses that will fit into a jam jar. Alternatively, you can just make the chilli-flavoured oil and this can be poured onto soft cheeses like Stracchino, Robbiola and even Philadelphia, but the idea behind preserving the cheese in oil was not only to flavour it but also to extend its viability.

You can use this recipe to preserve your cheeses in the traditional way, but you can also make it 3–4 days in advance of a dinner party as a starter, perhaps with some prosciutto di Parma on the side. The reason for using a jar is that they are easy to store and don't spill, but if the cheeses are going to be eaten in a few days' time, then another type of container will suffice so long as it is snug – otherwise you'll need loads of olive oil to cover the cheeses. Adjust the quantities to suit and allow at least 3 days for the flavours to infuse. SERVES 4 AS A STARTER

4 fresh Tomini cheeses from your local delicatessen *1 small bay leaf*
2 red chilli peppers, or more to taste! *a pinch of salt*
2 whole peppercorns *extra-virgin olive oil*
2 juniper berries

PLACE THE TOMINI CHEESES in a jam jar, making sure they are snug but not packed in too tightly. Usually four will fit into a ½ litre Bormioli preserving jar.

Chop the chillies. There is no need to remove all the seeds unless there is an excessive amount, as you want the heat to penetrate the oil and the cheese and the seeds can contain some considerable heat. Put all other ingredients into the jar and top up with the olive oil, gently shaking the jar to ensure that the cheeses are covered. Use a good olive oil as this is not just a medium for storing the cheeses but part of the flavour of the finished dish. If wished, other ingredients, such as herbs, could be added to flavour the oil a little, but the main ingredients are the cheeses, chillies and oil.

Store in the fridge but serve at room temperature otherwise the oil will be cloudy and thick. Always serve with good bread and wine, not water, to 'put out the flames', and certainly not with soft drinks or juice!

ZIA ANNA'S PRESERVED GREEN TOMATOES

This is a fantastic recipe for using up green tomatoes. The quantities will depend on the amount you have, so let this be an instruction rather than a recipe. Unlike a chutney, you can use preserved tomatoes straight away. They are quite sweet and sour, so great with porchetta (Roman roast pork with fennel seeds and garlic) or a good bread.

For every 2 kg green tomatoes you will need about 1 kg table salt, 3 onions, 3 celery sticks (both chopped chunkily), 250 ml average balsamic vinegar, sugar, olive oil

FIRST, CLEAN THE TOMS and cut them into nice meaty slices, without seeds. Then pour some salt into a large sieve and add the tomato slices together with more salt. Now put a weight on the whole tomato/salt thing. I use a clean container half full of water, but you could use a plate with a weight on it. Leave the tomatoes overnight to dry out, then wash them to remove the salt and let them dry on the draining board.

When they are dry, boil the onions, tomatoes and celery for 10 minutes in the vinegar. Put them into jars with a teaspoon of sugar and some salt to taste, as they will still need to be seasoned. Make sure you get in as much of the mixture as you can and tap it down, but leave a centimetre at the top so you can fill it with the olive oil. Put the lid on, turn the jar upside down and then let it settle again right side up so you can see if it needs a further top-up. Then simply seal the jars following the instructions on page 206.

ORANGE GRAPPA

The secret of this liqueur's wonderful wintry flavour is macerating the clove-studded orange.

30 cloves
1 medium organic orange
1 litre grappa or pure alcohol

400 ml of sugar syrup (240 g sugar dissolved in 400 ml simmering water, skimmed and allowed to cool)

STICK THE CLOVES IN THE ORANGE then place all the ingredients in a wide-necked bottle or container with a lid and leave to macerate for 14 days, stirring occasionally. Orange varieties will vary and the aim is to release the orange oils from the skin. I have found that some oranges take longer than others, so taste the liqueur to check the flavours. If it's not orangey enough then leave for longer, and if it's not sweet enough, add a little more sugar. When you are satisfied with the flavour decant into a bottle.

Nocino della Lina
LINA'S WALNUT LIQUEUR

When I want to sow something new or I have a general vegetable-growing question, I ring Lina – a no-fuss lady who worked the land, kept animals, made wine to sell, grew vegetables and understood the land like no other. When my father was a young man he saw Lina walking up the mountain with her gerla – a big wicker basket full of straw and wood. She was resting by the side of the road and my dad, wanting to be a gentleman, offered to carry the load the rest of the way. She declined but Dad insisted. He put the straps over his shoulders and tried to stand. He tried and tried, but to no avail; he just couldn't lift the basket. Lina, rested and amused, popped her arms through the straps, lifted the gerla as if it were empty, and steadily walked up the mountain to deliver the heavy load. She is old now and can't walk far, but she insists on sharing her knowledge of the land and she makes the best Nocino liqueur.

It is tradition that the walnuts must be collected on the night of San Giovanni Battista (St John the Baptist, 24 June). It was said that witches met under a walnut tree on this night to make their magic spells! The point is that picking them on this day works. They should be local walnuts and without any chemical treatments. The other tradition is that you must have an odd number of walnuts, though I don't know the origin of this, so use either 13 or 15, but never 14.

I have seen other ingredients being added to Nocino depending on who is making it and where they are from. These include lemon zest, some coffee beans, small amounts of cinnamon, rose water and a few cloves. Some recipes also mix water with the alcohol, but Lina doesn't use it and she's almost 90. Some recipes will add more sugar, some less, but try it this way and if it needs more sweetness to suit your palate, add more next time you make it.

This is a drink you prepare in the summer and enjoy at Christmas. Like a chutney or Christmas pudding, it needs to mature. It will be rough at first, but a couple of months in the cupboard and it will transform into a pleasing, smooth liqueur.

15 green walnuts, husks on
1 litre grappa or pure alcohol
500 g sugar

YOU'LL NEED A WIDE-NECKED 1.5–2 LITRE BOTTLE OR JAR with a lid for this recipe. Tradition calls for a container that has no rubber seals and, of course, make sure you have sterilized it.

Leave the walnuts on a sunny windowsill for two days before cutting them into quarters and adding them to the alcohol in the jar. This will improve the flavour of the Nocino.

Leave it to infuse for 60 days but not in a dark place as it must have partial sunlight. A sideboard or kitchen shelf would be fine. Occasionally open the jar and stir it.

After at least 60 days, filter the Nocino into dark bottles if possible, otherwise clear ones, and keep them in the dark until Christmas.

BROTH

To be able to make good broth or stock is really important as it is infinitely tastier than using a stock cube. A chicken should give you three meals – first you roast it, then you eat the leftovers cold with a nice chutney, and then you make broth with the bones and remaining meat. I find chicken stock excellent for making risotto; the flavour really lifts the whole dish.

My aunt Fiorina, who grew rice and kept chickens and who would eat risotto twice a day, always made her risotto with real broth. On the rare occasions she didn't have real broth (she also kept it in the freezer), she wouldn't bother making the risotto as it just wouldn't taste of anything.

You can use this stock in different ways – to make risotto, to make minestrone and soups, or just add some tortellini and reheat to make a classic Tortellini in Brodo, served with some toasted stale bread with a drizzle of olive oil and some grated Parmesan cheese.

1 chicken carcass
1 carrot, scraped
1 onion, peeled
1 celery stick

6–7 peppercorns
1 teaspoon salt
bouquet garni (optional)

PLACE THE CHICKEN IN A SAUCEPAN and cover it with water. If you have any meat left over, then put that in too – you can always make chicken and sweetcorn soup with your broth and the boiled chicken meat. This also goes for any bits left on the legs or wings.

Add the other ingredients and a bouquet garni if you have one, but this is not essential for making basic stock. Put everything in the pan and bring to a gentle simmer. When you see a foam forming on the top, just before simmering point, remove it with a spoon into a mug and keep going until the scum is almost gone (you won't get it all but you should be able to remove most of it).

Cover the broth and simmer on a low heat for 1 hour. Allow to cool a little then strain into a suitable container, retaining the onion, carrot and celery if you wish.

'Tutto fa brodo'

EVERYTHING MAKES BROTH

VINCENZO'S OLIVE FARCITE

When we first owned our deli, Dad would have big jars of plain olives in the fridge counter, but we couldn't give them away. Then he decided to marinate them and after that we couldn't stop them flying out of the deli and had to make them on a daily basis, though always to sell the following day as they are too harsh if served freshly made. These are very easy to prepare and I guarantee they will all disappear. The olives can be with or without stones, but without is better for eating on bread. If possible, don't use stuffed olives.

250 g green olives
250 g black olives
5 cloves of garlic, chopped (not crushed)
4 sun-dried tomatoes, chopped

5 anchovies, drained with oil reserved, chopped
2 tablespoons chopped parsley
extra-virgin olive oil
salt and freshly ground black pepper

PUT THE OLIVES into a large glass mixing bowl and add all the chopped ingredients. Pour in a slosh of olive oil together with the anchovy oil and stir until the olives are covered with the oils.

Taste an olive to check the seasoning and add salt and pepper to taste. At this point they will be strong and sharp, but cover and leave in the fridge overnight and the flavours will mix and become mellow, creamy and smooth. Serve at room temperature.

Polenta Dolce della Zia Angelina
ANGELINA'S SWEET POLENTA

This is my aunt Angelina's speciality della casa. She serves these lovely diamond-shaped cakes with meat main courses. They go especially well with the strong flavour of game, or with dishes that you would normally serve with a sweet sauce, like roast pork or lamb. SERVES 4–6

1 litre milk
175 g semolina
4 tablespoons sugar
a pinch of salt

zest of 1 lemon
4 eggs, separated
150 g breadcrumbs
oil for frying

HEAT THE MILK IN A PAN and, when warm, gradually stir in the semolina. Add the sugar and salt. Cook on a low heat for about 45 minutes. Remove from the heat and stir in the lemon zest and egg yolks. Grease a plate or a piece of marble and pour the mixture on to this to a thickness of about 3–4 cm and allow to cool.

Cut into diamond shapes, then dip each shape into the beaten egg white and breadcrumbs. Fry in oil until golden brown and leave to drain on kitchen paper. Serve immediately.

Bread Following a sharp decline in bread-making, many people (including me!) now have bread machines, there is a new appreciation of fresh, warm bread that has just come out of the 'oven' and some of the basics of bread-making are returning into our repertoires – a good thing.

Add the ingredients, set the timer, go away, and three hours later you have a hot, steamy loaf and the most divine aroma in the house. No, I'm not sponsored by the bread-machine manufacturers, but they have changed the way people look at bread. In fact, so successful have they been that flour sales are through the roof. They have even got people making bread by hand again, as after success with the machine they gain enthusiasm and decide to go that step further.

The machines are also labour saving in that you can set them just to make and knead the dough, and they do a very good job of it. You can then take this dough an hour and a half later, make it into the loaf shape you require, brush it with a salt or milk wash or sprinkle with seeds or cheese, and then stick it in the oven.

We often fill our machine with bread or brioche ingredients, set the timer overnight, and in the morning the whole house smells like a patisserie and we can't wait to get downstairs and eat our bounty with good butter and some homemade jam.

L'appetito con pane e Toma
e il cuoco migliore di Roma

BREAD AND TOMA [CHEESE FROM PIEDMONT] SATISFIES MORE THAN THE BEST MEAL IN ROME

Pane di Noci e Gorgonzola

GORGONZOLA AND WALNUT BREAD

This is a rustic loaf that will go well with a variety of savoury dishes or just on its own. The reason for having only a teaspoon of salt is that the Gorgonzola and mortadella are salty. Never be afraid to adjust the quantities slightly – some flours are thirstier than others so you may have to add some more water a little at a time, or more flour for that matter. The semolina gives this a nice 'toasted' flavour and a grainy texture, quite rustic. Make sure your packet of yeast weighs 9 g - some brands are only 7 g.

300 g strong white bread flour

170 g strong brown bread flour

30 g semolina

1 teaspoon salt

1 teaspoon sugar

1 sachet (9 g) yeast

2 tablespoons vegetable oil

250 ml water

50 g chopped walnuts (or to taste)

80 g Gorgonzola cheese

1 slice of mortadella, chopped

IF YOU'RE USING A BREAD MACHINE, put all the ingredients into your machine except the walnuts, Gorgonzola and mortadella, which you will add when your machine beeps (when the dough ball has been made and kneaded), so that they don't get completely crushed into the bread. Select the 750 g loaf setting and 'thick crust', if your machine has it, and off you go.

You could, if you like, use the dough-making setting and make the dough in the machine. Then place the dough on an oiled and floured baking tray in the shape that you like (a ball would be best) and cover loosely with a damp tea towel until it has doubled in size. Preheat the oven to Gas Mark 7/220°C. Place the loaf in the oven and bake for about 20 minutes until medium brown and hollow sounding when tapped underneath.

The third method is the traditional method of making the bread by hand. Mix all the dry ingredients except the walnuts, Gorgonzola and mortadella. Place the flour mixture on the table and make a well in the centre. Pour in the oil and water and start mixing from the inside out until you have a dough ball. You will have to knead the dough for at least 10 minutes to give the dough the elasticity it needs to rise and bake properly. Add the remaining ingredients and knead them into your dough for a further 2–3 minutes. You can test this elasticity by taking a piece of the dough and slowly stretching it in all directions: it shouldn't snap or break into holes.

Place the dough on a greased and floured baking tray, cover with a clean, damp tea towel and leave to rise in a warm place for about 1½ hours, until it has doubled in size. You could put it in a cold oven or microwave or in the airing cupboard, but the important thing is not to leave it in a draught, as this will affect how it rises. Preheat the oven to Gas Mark 7/220°C. Uncover the dough, dust with a little flour and put in the oven. Bake for about 20 minutes or until it is medium brown and sounds hollow when tapped.

PIZZA

Don't get me started. When I see what is offered under the name 'pizza', it makes me want to cry. There are so many cheap and nasty examples. The 'best' one I ever saw though nearly made me crash as I drove past an Indian restaurant that had the proud boast in the window 'Original Balti Pizza'. Also, you cannot microwave pizza. Glad we got that sorted out.

A home-made pizza is streets ahead of some other pizzas, which we all know and so I won't mention, but my message is that the Americans did not invent them, they're from Naples. In Naples, you can still buy pizza by the metre and how cool is that? One metre or two?

Pizzas are really straightforward to make as you don't need to leave the dough to rise. You simply mix the ingredients, knead (10 minutes by hand or with your bread machine) and roll it out. Put some mozzarella and tomato on the base and then the toppings of your choice. You can pile your pizza with as many toppings as you want and you can make them much healthier and better quality than shop-bought pizzas. This is one of those times when canned tomato is better than fresh for the base, though you can put fresh on as a topping.

You can use normal fast-acting bread-making yeast, but if you go to your deli and ask for pizza yeast, they will usually be able to supply it – it is a raising agent rather than a yeast. MAKES 2 LARGE PIZZAS

450 g strong white bread flour	*1 teaspoon salt*
290 ml water	*1 sachet (9 g) pizza yeast or fast-acting*
2 tablespoons olive oil	*bread-making yeast*

IF YOU HAVE A BREAD MACHINE, add all the ingredients and use the 'dough' setting, which will mix and then knead the dough.

If doing it by hand, on a worktop or table, make a well in the middle of the dry ingredients, pour in the wet ingredients and mix all the ingredients together starting from the centre until you have a nice dough ball. Knead it for 10 minutes.

Preheat the oven to Gas Mark 7/220°C. You can use the dough straight away without letting it rise or rest. Divide into two or four balls and roll them out until you have a thin base. Home-made pizza can be oblong or square if you don't have a round pizza dish, by the way. You don't have to, but I like my bases nice and crispy, so I put them in the oven for 3–4 minutes before putting the toppings on.

The key thing is to always start with a tomato sauce (passata, tinned chopped tomatoes or a home-made tomato sauce), then the cheese, and then the toppings. In my opinion, Cheddar is superb on pizza because of its strong flavour. Yes, not very traditional, but exceptions can be made for good taste!

I'm not sure how you learn these things but you just know the order in which things go on top of a pizza. So you wouldn't put ham and then onion, but onion and then ham. Capers and olives always go last, as do anchovies. You don't put cheese on fish pizzas. With bresaola and rocket pizza, these two ingredients go on raw after the pizza is cooked. Anchovies go with both meat and fish pizzas. Black olives on pizza, not green. Beer with pizza, not wine.

I usually put tomato, cheese (Cheddar and mozzarella) and some sliced red onion, and then my other ingredients can be varied. I made pizzas last night and we added some mortadella and capers and served the pizzas with a drizzle of chilli oil.

BUTTER 'FATTA IN CASA'

One of the easiest things you can make yourself at home, if not with a little arm work, is butter. Home-made butter tastes really nice for eating fresh on bread, but doesn't cook as well as the shop-bought stuff, which has a higher fat content and hence contains less water. You can flavour the butter with garlic and parsley or herbs like chives or sage at the sieving stage when the butter is soft and pliable.

500 ml single cream
salt
2 tablespoons water

THE ONLY EQUIPMENT YOU NEED FOR THIS is a big jar with a wide neck and a lid that closes tight. Pour some boiling water into it first to sterilize it. You simply pour the cream into the jar and add a good pinch of salt and the water.

Then you shake really hard up and down so that the contents 'hit' against the base and the lid. You shake and you shake and you shake the jar until your arms feel they are going to fall off! What will happen is that the contents will become thick and you will think that you are never ever going to end up with butter. But then, as if by miracle, the mixture separates and you are left with a solid lump of butter (still with lots of moisture in it) and with buttermilk, which is great for making pancakes.

Strain the buttermilk and keep it in the fridge for up to three days. Place the butter in a fine sieve. Press it down with a wooden spatula and jiggle it about in the sieve for about 5 minutes to get rid of as much of the excess liquid as you can. Then use the spatula to slap it into little tablets or bars before popping them into the fridge.

Castagne con Miele e Panna

HONEYED CHESTNUTS WITH CREAM

A classic of the Valle d'Aosta, the highest region of Italy, where all the ingredients are found naturally. Use good honey for this dish and if you cannot get clotted cream, use fresh whipped cream. Don't use spray cream – cream comes from cows not cans. SERVES 4

24–28 chestnuts, but cook a few extra as there are always bad ones!
1 teaspoon salt
clotted cream

alpine or white unsalted butter
3 tablespoons mountain honey
Calvados or brandy (optional)
1 bottle Moscato wine

OFTEN CHESTNUTS ARE BOILED in well-salted water, but as this is a sweet dish we are going to reduce the salt. The chestnuts can be cooked a day earlier, if preferred. Pierce with a sharp knife and put into a saucepan of boiling water together with the salt. Boil for 10 minutes, or until a skewer goes through easily. Chestnuts vary in size so test a large one to make sure. Allow to cool a little and then peel.

Before you start cooking the dish, put the cream into a nice bowl, which everyone will dip into. And make sure the wine is chilled.

Melt some butter in a heavy pan and throw the chestnuts in to heat through for a few minutes on a medium heat. Add the honey. The chestnuts will start to colour, so to stop them burning, turn the heat down and add a teaspoon of water or even Calvados or brandy and reduce the dressing down to a thick, sticky coating.

To serve, place the chestnuts in a plate and allow guests to take them at will and scoop them into the cream. The hot chestnuts will melt the edge of the cream and leave guests licking their fingers.

The chilled Muscat wine complements the dish perfectly and is part of this mountain tradition.

'Non dimenticare castagne per I morti'

DON'T FORGET CHESTNUTS FOR ALL SOULS' DAY

PIERINO'S 'SUN-DRIED' FIGS

A friend's mum, who lived in an apartment in Turin, used to make these and they are just amazing. They won't keep for long both in terms of shelf life and because they are so delicious they'll get scoffed up. This is a good way to get children eating figs, which are full of fibre, but make sure they don't eat too many, for obvious reasons!

almonds (the same number as you have figs)   *honey*
figs   *fennel seeds*

GENTLY ROAST THE ALMONDS in a dry pan until they are golden brown but not burnt, or they will taste bitter. Then simply cut each fig in half and place an almond inside with a couple of fennel seeds and drizzle the outside with a little honey, some of which will, of course, seep inside too. Cook them in a very mild oven at about Gas Mark ½ /100°C for about 1 hour and allow to cool.

KATY'S CARNIVAL BUGIE

Carnival is important in Italy and is held in February. The most famous is probably the one held in Venice, although every village, town and city in Italy also celebrates its own saint and has a meal or festa to honour them. In our village the patron saint is San Lorenzo (St Lawrence) and he is celebrated with nine nights delle stelle cadenti, of the shooting stars, with a speciality dish every single night, dancing, fireworks, fairground rides and drinking lots of local wine.

Bugie are eaten in Piedmont on Shrove Tuesday. They are very simple, but moreish, and should be served with Asti Spumante or Prosecco.

180 g butter   *2 sachets of Pane degli Angeli or Bertolini vanilla*
300 g sugar   *yeast, available from Italian delis*
6 eggs   *zest of 1 lemon*
1 glass milk or wine   *oil for frying*
1 kg plain flour, sifted   *icing sugar, sifted*
    salt

MIX THE BUTTER AND SUGAR TOGETHER and then add the eggs. When you have a nice mixture mix in the milk or wine. Add the flour, yeast, some salt, and then the lemon zest to form a soft dough.

Roll out to 2 cm thickness, cut into strips with a pasta/pastry cutter and shallow fry until golden but not dark brown in colour. Remove with a slotted spoon, drain on kitchen paper, and sprinkle with sifted icing sugar before serving warm.

BURNT SUGAR AND LEMON CAKE

This cake is not sweet – the lemon and burnt sugar make it pleasantly bitter. Even my four year-old son likes it served with fresh strawberries or ice cream and it is pleasing at the end of a meal with coffee or an Asti Spumante as it is not too rich. I like this straightforward type of cake mix, where you just mix the ingredients together and put them in the oven.

300 g self-raising flour

50 g polenta flour

100 g butter, melted

120 g sugar

4 capfuls of Marsala or sherry

250 ml milk

zest of 1 lemon

4 eggs

1 sachet of Pane degli Angeli or Bertolini vanilla
    yeast from your Italian deli, or 2 teaspoons
    baking powder and 1 teaspoon natural vanilla
    extract

60 g dark muscovado sugar

fresh strawberries and ice cream (optional) to serve

THOROUGHLY MIX ALL THE INGREDIENTS, except the muscovado sugar and the strawberries, using a balloon whisk. It doesn't matter if there are a few small lumps – it doesn't have to be completely smooth. Put into a suitable cake tin, which you have greased with some butter and floured. The tin must be big enough to take the cake mix but not be more than two-thirds full or less than half full.

The beauty of muscovado sugar is that it forms lumps. Place the lumps evenly on top of the cake (but don't be too formal about it). Some of the lumps will be larger and some will crumble – it doesn't matter. They will melt and caramelize, forming a wonderful bitter-sweet contrast. Bake at Gas Mark 4/180°C for about 30 minutes. Test by inserting a knife into the part that has risen the highest. If the knife comes out clean, it is cooked. If not, pop it back in for 5 minutes more.

Allow to cool in the dish until lukewarm before removing. You may find that some of the sugar has drizzled down the sides into the cake, fusing with the dish, so just cut around the edge of the cake before removing rather than risk breaking the cake in the process.

Frittelle di Mele
APPLE FRITTERS

Trust me, everyone will love these, bambini and big bambini alike. SERVES 4

1 large egg
4 tablespoons flour
1 tablespoon sugar
fennel seeds to taste
100 ml milk

3 apples
vegetable oil for shallow frying
butter
sugar

FIRST MAKE THE BATTER by breaking the egg into a bowl and mixing in the flour, sugar and fennel seeds. Start adding some milk and mixing it in – there's no real quantity on the milk. You just need a 'pastella' (batter) that is thick enough to coat the apples but doesn't drop off as soon as you pick them up.

Peel and core the apples and cut them into rings – not too thin or you'll have apple crisps! Put some vegetable oil with a knob of butter in a frying pan and heat until quite hot, then turn it down a little or the butter will burn. Get a plate ready with some kitchen paper in it while the pan is heating up. Dip each apple ring in the batter and put into the hot pan, frying on each side until they are light brown. Lift out and put on to the kitchen paper to absorb a little of the oil so they're not too greasy. Sprinkle with sugar and serve straight away with a glass of Moscato wine.

Torta di Pane
BREAD CAKE by Lina Stores, Soho

200 g breadcrumbs
100 g Amaretti biscuits, crushed
150 g sugar
2 eggs, beaten
200 ml cooking cream
1 glass Martini Rosso

100 g cooking chocolate, finely chopped
½ glass of milk
1 sachet of Bertolini or Pane degli Angeli vanilla
*   yeast from your Italian deli*
vanilla sugar for dusting

PUT ALL THE INGREDIENTS APART FROM THE VANILLA SUGAR into a bowl and mix until thoroughly amalgamated. Pour into a well-greased and floured 22 cm cake tin. Bake at Gas Mark 4/180°C for 40 minutes. Turn out on to a cooling rack and, when cool, dust with vanilla sugar. Serve by cutting into pretty diamond-shaped pieces.